A JOURNEY TO LAKE MANSAROVARA

(in Undes, a Province of Tibet)

WILLIAM MOORCROFT

Introduction by

H.T. Colebrooke

Edited with a Preface by
J. L. GUPTA

GIAN PUBLISHING HOUSE
DELHI - 7

GIAN PUBLISHING HOUSE
29/6 Shakti Nagar, Delhi-110007

ISBN 81-212-0101-2

PRINTED IN INDIA

Published by Gian Publishing House, Delhi (India) and
Printed by Godwall Printers, Delhi

EDITOR'S PREFACE

TO write some prefatory lines to the book *A Journey to Lake Mansarovara* we feel pleasure to acquaint the readers with the general thematic viewpoint maintained or rather set in the book. The present format of the book is an edited and revised version and not the facsimile reproduction of what had originally been written by William Moorcroft, the narrator as well as the author. As the entire story was already published straightforwardly, it has been chapterised in the present book-form with some editorial modifications. The original text has not at all been interferred except some improvement in retaining symetry in style and uniformity in spellings and punctuation. Every possible effort has been made to bring the book upto the mark keeping in mind the convenience of the readers.

To start with, this is an adventurous journey/odyssey undertaken by the author himself, his colleagues and a few others whom they met on their journey to the lake Mansarovara, the place of much reverence and attraction due to its several unique qualities and scenic beauties. Initially a band of three persons as already mentioned, sets out on their journey, not with some specific intention in their mind but just to reach their difficult and unattainable goal with good and pious motives to explore the unique and landscapic beauties of the lake with which it is gifted, and to know about the inhabitants residing there intact of the society. They continue their journey enthusiastically but ungrudgingly, arrive at different places, big and small, cross many cliffs and mountains facing the hardships as well as narrating the incidents they frequently came across. In this study many a time, we come across some lines which describe different types of inhabitants and the characteristics of their customs, rites and vegetations grown around those places.

The adventurers meet many people who are unknown to them. They talk with them and try to justify the pious cause of their journey while they are debarred from going onwards on the suspicion of there being *Firungis*. They had to overcome many critical and juncturous situations satisfying their opponents in rational way and protecting themselves.

To sum up, the book clearly gives many instances to elucidate that journey undertaken throws much light and invites attention of the reader towards the courageous mood of the odyssey-makers, the landscapic beauties of the high mountains covered with snow, rivers having swift, cold and clear waters. It presents vivid picture of trees, vegetations grown around and sudden and unexpected climatic conditions prevailing there. There are also many references to people whom the travellers met at different places at different times, describing their strange habits, customs and rites. The journey is, in fact, rich with a vast collection of knowledge which is related to socio-economic and political aspects of the inhabitants living there in the mountains and ridges. It will be no exaggeration if it is called an explorative journey to Lake Mansarovara.

We sincerely hope that this book will certainly arouse curiosity and interest in the reader if a portion of the book is gone through. Since it, provides a panoramic view of all those things and curios the travellers saw on their way, we think this book will, of course, enthrall readers and captivate them to go deep into the study to know the rich Himalayan culture and heritage.

July 1987 J.L. GUPTA.

INTRODUCTION

I have much gratification in being enabled to lay before the Society, an extract from the journal of our colleague, Mr. Moorcroft, on a journey to explore that part of little *Tibet* in *Chinese Tartary*, where the shawl goat is pastured; and to visit the celebrated lake *Mansarovara* or *Mapang*, in which the *Ganges* was long supposed to take its source.

Undertaken from motives of public zeal, to open to *Great Britain* means of obtaining the materials of the finest woollen fabric, the arduous and perilous enterprise in which Mr. Moorcroft, accompanied by Captain Hearsay, engaged, and which was prosecuted by them with indefatigable perseverance and admirable intrepidity, undismayed by the difficulties of the way and the dangers with which the jealousy of the *Nepalese* beset them on their return, and undeterred by hardships and privations, and in Mr. Moorcroft's instance by frequent illness, has in the result not only accomplished the primary object which was in view, but has brought an interesting accession of knowledge of a country never before explored; and has ascertained the existence, and approximately determined the situation of *Mansarovara*, verifying at the same time the fact, that it gives origin neither to the *Ganges*, nor to any other of the reputed rivers to flow from it. Mr. Moorcroft, as will be seen, found reason to believe that the lake has no outlet. His stay, however, was too short to allow of his making a complete circuit of it : and adverting to the difficulty of conceiving the evaporation of the lake's surface in so cold a climate to be equivalent to the influx of water in the season of thaw from the surrounding mountains, it may be conjectured, that, although no river run from it, nor any outlet appear at the level at which it was seen by Mr. Moorcroft, it may have some drain of its superfluous waters, when more slown, and at its greatest elevation, and may then, perhaps, communicate with *Rawan* lake, (in which the *Setlej* takes its source) conformably with the oral information received by our travellers.

The journal of the entire route, from their departure from the *British* frontier in *Rohilkhand*, to their return, being more copious than would consist with the limits of the volume of our researches, I have used the liberty of selection, which Mr. Moorcroft has liberally allowed, and confined the extract of the journal to that part of the route which is wholly novel ; at the same time curtailing the narrative, though with regret, for the unavoidable exclusion of many interesting passages. It is proper, however, to observe, that no other freedom has been used ; and that the narrator's own words are scrupulously retained.

H.T. GOLEBROOKE

CONTENTS

Editor's Preface v

Introduction vii

1. Journey to Lake Mansarovara : May 26th to May 31st 1
2. Journey to Lake Mansarovara : June 1st to June 30th 11
3. Journey to Lake Mansarovara : July 1st to July 31st 35
4. Journey to Lake Mansarovara : August 1st to August 31st
5. Journey to Lake Mansarovara : The Month of September 104
6. Journey to Lake Mansarovara : The Month of October 120

Index 141

1

JOURNEY TO LAKE MANSAROVAR : MAY 26 TO MAY 31ST

May 26th.—At *Joshi-Math* we left the road to *Bhadrinath*, which crosses the *Dauli* a little more than a cos above the town. At the junction of the *Vishnu-Ganga* with the *Dauli*, both rivers lose their names and the united streams form the *Alacananda*, the course of which has been before mentioned. As the road to *Joshi-Math* is known by the surveys of the gentlemen deputed by Colonel Colebrooke, I have not been very particular in describing it[1] but, as the road to *Niti* and onwards is new ground to Europeans, I shall follow it with more exactness.

The principal part of the minutes of our route is taken from the note book of Mr. Hearsay who carried the compass and brought up the rear, accompanied by Harkh Dev, and who engaged on setting out to execute this part. Harkh Dev Pandit was directed to stride the whole of the road at paces equal to 4 feet each.[2]

---

1. For the same reason it is omitted in this abridgment. C.

2. The *Pandit's* measure of the road would probably have been more correct, had he been directed to step his usual and natural paces, the length of which might have been easily determined with precision by a small trial. C.

Our road lay along the left bank of the *Dauli*, but generally at the distance of at least a cos. The road was pleasant but the heat was greater than might have been expected, seeing that the summits of the mountains very near us were covered with snow.

The road was frequently crossed by small streams of water, of which several issue from stone conduits now out of repair. We saw people sowing the *Lal Sag* or Amaranthus Gangeticus, a vegetable apparently much used by the mountaineers.

Wheat was nearly ready to cut and lands under the plough. The ears of the wheat particularly long and bearded.

About a cos before we reached the ground for encampment, we met our carriers returning, who said that they had executed their task but had received neither victuals nor money. It appears to me that the *Chaudri* of *Joshi Math*, who received our advances and undertook to supply the people, will keep the whole money for his own use, and press the unfortunate villagers to carry our baggage.

Some mountains near us, whose tops were covered with snow when we first came, were in the evening nearly bare.

At half past eleven reached the town of *Baragaon*, and not finding good shade went on higher, above three quarters of a mile, without being much more successful.

The cultivated lands, in the middle of which is the village of *Baragaon*, run half way up the hill where the forest region begins with small trees, becoming thicker and higher as it ascends and the very summit is fringed with pines and the majestic and fine overtopping cedar.[3]

27th.—In the afternoon the *Negi* came to say that on the following morning, he would have people to take our baggage to *Tapoban* a village about three cos distant, from whence we should proceed onwards the following day.

28th.—Resume our journey, leaving our ground at 6.30 therm. sunrise 58°. Pass by a *Sanga* over the *Dauli*, and at 3696 paces reach our ground, a little below the almost deserted village of *Tapoban*, placed on the brow of a hill surmounted

3. Pinus Deodar and Longifolia.

by woods of pine, cedar and cypress.[4] A considerable stream falls into the *Dauli* below the village ; and by the side of this is a small rivulet of tepid water. This current mixes with the cold stream before it reaches the *Dauli* and issues from some rough ground in the face of a rock. The heat of the water seemed to be very agreeable to tadpoles which had deserted the colder stream to take refuge in this.

I observed a common plant something resembling butcher's-broom, which was said to be the *Setbarua* from which the mountaineers make a paper that is sold at *Sirinagar* and *Almora*, and from thence finds its way into *Hindustan*, although not in large quantities. The bankers employ it for their bills of exchange or *Hundis*, in preference to any other kind, as the ink does not sink further into its substance than is necessary to retain the writing, as it does not imbibe water readily and relatively to its thickness is much stronger than any other kind of paper. As connected with paper, I must here observe, that the layers of the bark of birch are used by the natives to write upon and they bear both ink and the stroke of the pencil very well. The leaves are called *Bhojpatr*. The bark of the birch is used at *Lacknau* for covering the wires of huka-snakes.

29th.—Settle to give Jowar Singh 26 rupees, in full of all taxes and demands to be made upon us until we reach the frontier, for which he gave a receipt on birch paper having previously put aside a fee of five rupees for the part he bore in the transaction. As our carriers came in a very straggling manner from the villages whence they had been pressed, we could not leave the ground till 8. At 6816 paces reach a hut taken possession of by our servants. This is computed to be seven cos from *Tapoban*.

After having reached the top of the first mountain, Mr. Hearsay who had gone before me, killed a very thin yellow snake about 18 inches in length. I found it had the poisonous fang but it is asserted that snakes and all other venomous reptiles, are very scarce in this part of the country. However,

---

4. Probably a species of pine, as well as that which Mr. Moorcroft denominates cedar. C.

on taking up the carpet on which I had slept, a black scorpion came from under it.

A warm spring which we passed early in this day's march, issues from the rock on the right of the road in a stream of about five inches across, and three deep, and threw up a small cloud of stream. At its escape the heat was so great that the finger could not bear being dipped in it more than 2 or 3 seconds. The thermometer having been carried forwards, we were prevented from ascertaining the temperature however, no insects were in it or about it and some plants which had fallen into it near the middle of the current, were killed and seemed parboiled. The pebbles in its bed and the vegetable substances which were immersed in it, were covered with a yellow coat, and those which had been taken out and become dry, were likewise coated with a white earthy substance, having little taste ; however, the water itself was slightly austere and I apprehend contained iron without any other mixture. The tepid stream at *Tapoban*, which is much lower and not half a mile distant, probably proceeds from the same source with this, and is cooled in it progress to the place at which it escapes below. I saw no appearance of volcano in this or any other mountain which I have yet met with but many abound with minerals and pyrites is found in great abundance.

Close to this place the road was broken by a recent slip and we had to pass upon the crumbling surface. The road this day was in many parts very fatiguing. In one place a slip of earth had laid bare a large surface of rock which had been formerly covered by the road and as it sloped to the river with a sharp descent, it required every exertion and care to guard against a slip of about a hundred feet into a current, which dashed with great force amongst fragments of marble, which in two or three points actually formed a bridge across the stream. In another part we were obliged to climb up the face of a rock nearly perpendicular, and on which irregularities for the toe to hang upon, were at a most inconvenient distance. My left foot having slipped off one of them, I lay for a few seconds upon the poise, but a snatch at a clump of grass which on being seized, luckily did not give way and a sudden spring brought me to a comparatively safe spot, with the loss of some skin from my knees and elbows and some rents in my trowsers and sleeves. Sometimes points of rock projected to the edge of the river and these were turned by rude staircases made of wood and stone. Retiring angles were passed by inclined planes formed by a tree being laid on points of stone on each side of the angle and loose stones were thrown from the wood to the rock. For a moment the eye could not quit the road and suffer the feet to proceed, without risk of accidents, and yet a trifling expense would render the road in general passable although it would always be liable to be injured by the falling of the rocks above.

When we had reached the custom-house on the middle of the mountain immediately beyond a *Sanga* by which we crossed the *Rauni,* we found one of our sircars who was detained by three men and as many women, as pledge for the payment of duties on the passage of our baggage. The receipt written upon a slip of birch bark was no sooner beheld by the most riotous of the men than he ceased to attempt any further molestation although it was clear that he had not read its contents. As however, one fellow was still a little impertinent, my friend insisted upon his relieving a carrier from his load, which he actually took part of the way up the hill and then slipping from under the load slid down a face of rock and, though old, skipped away from point to point of a rough road with the agility of a deer. As many loads were left behind, it was deemed prudent to take the third man along with us as an hostage for their safe passage. As he went along, he told us that the *Chaudri Calyan* had farmed the customs of this place for 500 rupees a year and that the woman who was so clamorous, was one of his wives, of whom he had seventeen. The other two women were her slaves.

To a poor woman who had much difficulty in carrying her burden over a very rough road, I gave a *Timasha* which in a few minutes was taken away from her by a man whom I supposed to be her husband. On learning that he was no relation, I got it from him, sent him about his business and returned the coin to the woman, but when she departed, I had the mortification of observing him at a considerable distance start from a place of concealment and again force the money from her. This man was a *Zemindar* of the village in which the poor woman lived and though he had been obliged by the *Negi* to carry a load, he still exercised his petty tyranny over one more defenceless than himself.

The gratification of the calls of hunger seems to be the first object amongst the inhabitants of a country which, if under a well regulated government, would be capable of exporting a surplus of provisions. At *Tapoban*, a stout young fellow offered himself to be my slave for life if I would only feed him. Although I wanted not his services and did not much like his appearance yet his appeal was too forcible to be resisted and I, therefore, engaged to give him food for his services.

30th.—Obliged to halt for the purpose of collecting carriers, which was difficult as the villages in this part of the country are small and distant from each other.

31st.—As this day my companion and myself separated and he had along with him the compass and the young Pandit who measured the road, I shall make extracts from his notes of the route, and afterwards notice my deviation from it. 'At 1381 paces ; tops of mountains covered with snow in every direction. At 2297, cross a rivulet which comes from E. Snowy mountains in that direction quite close. At 2437, commence ascending the most tremendous place I ever saw. At 2783, descend to the bed of *Dauli* river, most thankful that I am once more safe : I was obliged to take off shoes and stockings. At 7610, reach our halting place. Ten hours upon the march. The coolies, mostly women, arrived at the same time. The *Dauli* much reduced in breadth but the current very strong with a small exception, its general course has been to the S.W.

I left our ground at 40 minutes past 5. From the bridges across the *Dauli*, having been swept away last year, and not reinstated, a new road has been made by the goat-herds along the sides and over the tops of the mountains which overlook the river. This has been first worked into a track by the goats and in the worst places strengthened by fragments of stones thrown in heaps somewhat imitating rude flights of steps. The path in various places formed by pieces of stone which jut out, overhangs the edge of the water and seldom retires so far from it as to give a chance of the traveller escaping from rolling down to the river, should he have the misfortune to make a false step, and the footing was very insecure from small stones being mixed with much loose earth. Just on attaining the summit I met a large flock of goats loaded, and was glad to find a secure corner until the whole had passed. I observed that goats when laden climb up places however apparently difficult without hesitation, but they do not like to go down steep declivities for whether they descend straight down or sideways, the load urges them forward quicker than they like, and as there is no belly-band, it frequently tumbles off and is the cause of the animal being carried down the steep sides of hills and lost. Goats cast a look of inquiry at strangers and pass on leisurely, but sheep generally stop, and after one has either been driven onwards or gone of his own accord, the rest follow with precipitancy and frequently lose their loads by their hurry.

Crossing this mountain took up an hour and a quarter. Having mounted a height which, though short, was steep and rugged, I was somewhat confounded by the sight of a steep and bare slope of stone, about 100 feet deep, running to the bed of the river without any path, and with a surface so smooth as to excite a doubt whether I could reach the bottom in any other way than by sliding, which would have been too rapid to be safe, the more especially as the stop must have taken place amongst stones in the bed of the river. By taking off my stockings, pressing the spike of my staff into little dips in the stone and catching at a friendly tuft of grass which occasionally presented itself near one edge, I got to the base nearly at the same time with the old Pandit whose activity would have more surprised me had I not known that he had been bred in the mountains of *Kamaon*. Just as we had congratulated ourselves on our escape, we saw two other paths, one higher up and another lower down under a ledge of the rock, which saved the rest of our party, save two of the Pandit's hill people, from the dangers of this road.

Soon after descending the slope, I overtook a woman who

had been pressed by the *Negi* to carry a load. She said that her measure of misery was full and that she was resolved to emigrate into *Jawar* where oppression was not so grievous as here.

Seeing our carriers who had started about three-quarters of an hour before me, supporting themselves on the ledge of a rock, which overhung the river at a great height, by clinging with their hands to the stones on the face of the mountain, and that at length they actually stopped, I was induced to make the experiment of going round by a winding path, under an idea that I should effect it in nearly as little time as would be spent in passing over the broken path of rock. Mr. Hearsay coming after me and finding that the carriers preferred the short, but more dangerous road, to the long one, resolved to attempt it, and assuredly I should have done the same, had I known the length and roughness of that which I actually took. Mr. Hearsay and a large portion of the carriers went over the rock without accident, but at one point the courage of my *Khansaman* failed ; for on missing footing with one leg, he shrieked violently and sunk down almost senseless upon a point of stone with one leg hanging down over the abyss, calling out that he was lost. Mr. Hearsay was at hand and assisted him most opportunely, along with the Pandit. One woman carried four burdens at different times for her less courageous companions and a bearer was also of some use, but at length became so alarmed as only to be capable of proceeding by being steadied by an end of his turban being tied round his waist and the other end secured by the young Pandit as he proceeded in front.

The horrors of this road were very great and ought so to have been to justify passing by such a road as that which I followed. For it cost me the labour of two hours to attain the top of the first mountain which I had to scale and although the path consisted of lines of zigzag, not more than 10 or 12 feet in length, at angles so sharp, that in a length of 24 feet, not more than 10 feet were gained in actual ascent, yet even this progress was not made except by clinging with the hands to shrubs, roots of trees, clumps of grass and clods of earth, and sometimes from the obliquity of the path, required me to creep on hands and knees to prevent slipping. Near the summit of the mountain, the path divided and a mountaineer whom we met, as we thought opportunely, at this point advised the lower one, though from the accounts of porters and servants who took the upper one, the latter was easier but a little longer.

In descending the mountain, a grand view opened from the S.E., consisting of a vista formed by two sides of mountains composing a glen, down which ran a large stream. One slope was enriched by a forest which reached to the clouds, the other covered by scanty pasturage for about 400 yards ; when it was overhung by a steep face of barren rock of immense height, and the upper part of the vale was shut up by a peak of still higher mountain, the base of which was sprinkled with cypress and the top whitened with snow.

After a tedious march of two hours more through a forest of cedars and cypress[5], of which many would have been large enough for main-masts of first rates, I came to a *Sanga* across the stream which ran down the valley. From this point I ascended the hill surmounted by the bare sheet of rock, by a goat path and had to cross an avalanche which was scarcely settled ; every now and then a piece of stone rolling down its face and bringing with it currents of earth. The path was narrow, occasionally going over a surface a little rounded, which, in some slight degree masked the tremendous declivity below and sometimes skirting its very verge. At one spot, on a ledge of rock, the old Pandit hesitated and retired into a hollow. However, having the advance he summoned up courage and passed the cause of his fears ; this was formed by an angular piece of rock having slipped out of the ledge or cornice on which we were walking and a piece of stone, which just, and only just, rested with both ends on the opposite edges of the gap, shewed a precipice of a depth sufficient to alarm the anxiety of a person who had not been much accustomed to the mountainous paths of this country. After clambering over fragments of stone which had fallen

5. Pines, see a former note.

from the heights, we came to a point of rock whence we had a complete view of the declivity over which we had to pass and this part was to me more difficult than any other. However, I reached the bottom of the hill without injury. I learnt that I had gone 4 cos, and had not made above half a mile of head way. From the fatigue of this detour, I was so enfeebled as to be under the necessity of halting five or six times in ascending a steep mountain and obliged to creep on my hands and knees for a great distance, not having sufficient confidence in my legs. My knees tottered and I was frequently attacked with such a violent pain in the right knee, as for a second or two almost deprived me of the use of the limb. I much suspect that I had lost my road. In creeping along I certainly made a wrong choice, as I found myself at once upon the brink of a precipice on the very angle of a rock which overhung it and a slit in the stone shewed me my danger at the very moment I was about to place my hand upon a fragment which the weight would probably have dislodged and carried me along with it ; at this moment the recollection of the danger produces an involuntary shiver. After some time I got into a tolerably good path and found my companion and the greatest part of the party, waiting my arrival by the side of a cool stream of excellent water.

The latter part of our march was not good, but this road although almost every where else it would have been deemed impassable except for goats, was good in comparison with that which constituted the labour of the morning. This has certainly been the most severe day's work we have had and yet I compute the actual distance, including the 4 cos of detour, cannot have exceeding 13 cos.

The ordinary road is not particularly difficult or dangerous and all the risk of life which I have mentioned, inconvenience to the inhabitants of the country and impediment to commerce are created for want of *Sangas* which might be made for 100 rupees, but the present government does nothing to ameliorate the state of the country or to increase the happiness of its subjects in these districts.

2

JOURNEY TO LAKE MANSAROVAR : JUNE 1ST TO JUNE 30TH

June 1st.—Commenced our march at 7.30. At 2345 paces the river becomes a succession of rapids, and has its channel diminished to about 20 yards in breadth. At 3407 paces we pass two caves, a small and a large one. The *Dauli* about eighteen yards broad. At 10,971 paces come to some cedars[1] and halt. The *Dauli* much reduced.

At our place of encampment, a black scorpion was brought and was said to be harmless ; however on pulling off his sting and pressing it, a large drop of a thin milk-coloured fluid escaped from its point.

On the top of a high mountain, thinly sprinkled with wormwood, dwarf cypresses,[1] and a kind of furze, blocks of marble and hard stones were scattered about in every direction, which seemed to contain minerals, and I am much deceived if I did not see some veins of silver[2] in strata of quartz. I had no instruments to break stones with nor did I see any small fragments which I could with convenience place in my girdle. I was obliged therefore rather to leave this point unsettled than

1. Pines.
2. Perhaps Mica. C.

to expose myself to the suspicion of coming into the country in search of precious metals. The surfaces of many of the hardest stones, on this side of the *Paie-kande*, are studded with small red crystals, which project ; at first view, one is disposed to take them for garnets but they are not transparent. They are so firmly imbedded in the substance of the stone which serves as matrix to them that they cannot be raised by any common instrument in a perfect state so that I could not count their faces.

The scenery of this day has always been wild and in some places most imposingly majestic, especially from the side of the mountain where we halted. On every side the view is bounded by summits of mountains peaked, rounded, broken into ascending and descending lines with abrupt ragged dips and a few soft hollow sweeps, but all covered with snow. The declivities in some parts thickly covered with cedars and cypresses[3], in others thinly sprinkled, and in others diversified by bare patches of rock or sand. The base of two lines of mountains is washed by the *Dauli* which runs with great rapidity and noise, about 400 feet below our encampment in a space only just large enough to receive the water which it now rolls along the channel. One slope of the hill immediately before us has been broken from top to bottom by a slip which has only lately happened. In its course it has overwhelmed large trees, of which some have been hurried into the river, others lay across its bed half buried in rubbish and others, thrown down, hang by their roots with their heads towards the base of the mountain. The devastation committed by large slips, is sometimes very great, and they frequently happen, for I have this instant heard a tremendous crash at a distance produced by a fall of rock and was awakened by another at a moment that I had lost all sense of fatigue under the shade of a large mass of stone.

When the structure of the exposed faces of mountains has not been entirely broken, I have remarked that the general direction of the component layers has been to the E. of N. with an inclination towards the horizon about the angle of 45°.

---

3. See a former note.

We pitched in an open space between two ranges of high rocks. At the foot were some large cedars.[4] I measured one at six feet from the ground, twentytwo feet in circumference.

This evening the report ran that a carrier had fallen off the first Sankho in this day's march, into the river with his load and was drowned.

June 2nd.—March at six with the same coolies. In one place the river is covered by masses of rock, under which the current rushes with great violence. At 350 paces we cross to the left bank of the river over a Sankho, consisting of three parts in consequence of two blocks of stone having fallen into the stream and formed three channels. It was in good order and thirty paces in length. At 4680 paces cross a broad large brook, in which there are large beds of frozen snow with a stream of water running beneath them, and immediately on the right bank of which is the village of *Malari.*

The road of today has exhibited much variety ; and a short account of its features will convey a general idea of those of this country. At first we passed over heaps of fragments of rocks ; afterwards over beds of pebbles ; then ascended a mountain partly by a path worn in the earth by frequent treading, and partly formed by the surface of rocks and by stairs : where the road on the face of the rock shelved much to the river, a few loose stones were laid upon it close to its edge ; and sometimes earth was thrown amongst them, or a few pine branches were placed along it and loaded with stones : this served as a kind of defence or parapet : but, as they were never higher than a foot from the level of the shelf, they would only stop a slip of the foot. Where niches were broken out of the rock in the line of the path, and formed gaps over the precipice, if only of small extent, a piece of wood was laid across the widest part, and slabs of such stone as was at hand laid from it to the rock, either supported by a ledge, or if the face of the rock chanced to be smooth, on another spar of wood. Where the gap was very wide, the trunk of a large tree was put across ; the upper side being cut a little flat, or

4. See a former note.

else having notches hewn in it as stepping places ; an open space being left between it and the wall. Commonly these trees or Sankhos over chasms, as well as those Sankhos across rivers, are tolerably well guarded against turning, either by being weighted with large stones at each end, or by having rude stone wedges driven through two holes at each extremity of the trunk or plank. Where the chasm is too long for a tree, a heap of flattish stones is placed in the nearest part, which affords room for the base of a flight of steps, constructed sometimes of stones wholly, sometimes of stones supported in front by logs of wood : but no railing is to be met with any where ; and from the general looseness of the mode of building, these roads are subject soon to get out of order ; but, if the stones be large and the base flat, this kind of stair lasts longer than might be expected, as the passengers walk with care. Slips from the hills do most mischief to them, and their course being almost always at the foot or on the side of mountains, exposes them to constant injury in some part of their extent. Today I had just crossed the slope of a slip that had happened last night ; when I heard a little trickling above, which rapidly increased, and was caused by a shower of small stones, of which some slid easily over the surface of the falling earth, but others, having got a little momentum by rolling over perpendicular breaks, dashed down with such force, as would have been fatal to any animal which they might have chanced to strike in their fall.

As Mr. Hearsay was following the coolies, three bears which were scampering up a steep gulley, that had been a watercourse, but was now half filled by sand, earth and stones, displaced stones about 300 feet above the road. These in their descent loosened others, and dashed across the road while the coolies were passing, but fortunately struck no one, except one of my bearers upon the leg, and he was more alarmed than hurt.

The view of the village of *Malari* from the top of the hill, where it comes in sight at a distance of about a mile, is pleasing and would give a good effect on canvass. It is placed in the eastern angle of a triangular plain about a mile on each face and bounded on two sides by streams, and on the other by steep hills, covered up to their summits with a bed of snow, thin on the projecting parts and deep in the ravines. The southern stream is half choked by banks of frozen snow, through which a mountain current, formed by spring-water and melted snow, forces its way, undermining the masses of congealed snow, which now impede its progress ; but which in two months will be dissolved and carried into the *Dauli* that runs with impetuosity from the north to the west.

The extremely neat state of the land recently sown principally with *Chena*,[5] and separated into fields by recently piled stone fences and living hedges, would do credit to any country ; but the proportion of cultivated to uncultivated land in this country, at present, is almost as a drop of water to a large river.

The village of *Malari* consists of about 20 houses, built of rough stones, cemented with clay, and mixed with much wood. Many are of one storey, but more of two, and some even of three storeys. The lower range is generally given to the cattle. Circular stones, with holes through the middle of them, are hung by ropes to the projecting ends of the beams at the gables, to prevent the roof being injured by gusts of wind which are here frequent and violent. The upper storey projects generally beyond the lower one, in consequence of its being furnished with a wooden verandah, which commonly runs along both sides, and is made of fir plank in strong pannels, ornamented with flowers and figures of *Hindu* deities, amongst which Ganesa is most frequently represented. There no lock, bolt, or latch to the doors, but in one door-post a square hole is cut, through which a rope is past, that ties a dog to it, who guards the entry with fidelity. His collar is of wood like a yoke collar, and a stick is tied to it, and likewise to the rope which holds him to the door.

Malari is inhabited by a class of people who call themselves *Rajput*, but appear to pay little attention to caste. The poorer class of inhabitants of the frontier eat raw meat with a little pepper and salt as seasoning ; which we had an opportunity

---

5. Panicum Miliaceum.

of seeing ; for the leg of a goat being thrown away in consequence of being tainted, the coolies instantly seized it, and made apparently a savoury meal from it. Both men and women are rather of low stature, but not ill made, and have something of the *Tartar* countenance mixed with that of the *Hindu*.

They dress in coarse woollen cloth made from the fleece of their own sheep, and of those of *Butan*. The women alone weave, sitting on the ground, and are very industrious and expert. In five days, with a very simple apparatus, a woman will weave a piece of cloth about 18 inches broad and 15 cubits long. This is called a *Pankhi*. Some of them are flat, but others are twilled and very strong. They are worn without being bleached or dyed. The proportion of females seems much greater than the males. This may be accounted for by part of the male population being taken by the *Nepalese* for their army, and by another part being engaged in going from the upper to the lower hilly district, to sell salt and bring back grain. The dress of both men and women is generally overrun with lice ; and their persons are with few exceptions, disgustingly filthy. The inside of the house is no less filthy than the dress of the inhabitants ; and as no other articles of furniture are to be seen in them than benches and cooking utensils, one might be led at first sight to believe, that the inhabitants laboured under the pressure of the severest poverty ; but this is not the case, as is shewn by the ornaments of the women ; and it is probable that they avoid making a display of wealth, lest it should be taken from them by the *Gorkhiahs* ; to which may be added the circumstance of their inhabiting this country only from about the 24th of May till the 23rd September, when they migrate to the villages of *Tapoban*, *Baragaon*, and other places to the N.E. of *Joshi-Math*. These people, from living half the year in one country and the remainder in another, are called *Dobasas*, and also *Marchas* ; which latter appellation gives a whimsical affinity in situation and name to the former inhabitants of the borders of *England* and *Scotland*. They carry on a considerable trade between the inhabitants of the *U'ndes* and those of the lower parts of the hills. From the former they procure borax and salt, which they either carry to the frontier of the Company's possessions or sell to the inhabitants of the hills and take back to *Butan* grain in exchange. This commerce produces a profit to the *Marchas* of at least a hundred per cent on the grain and about 150 or 200 on the salt, but can only be carried on during the six months of the year when they reside on the *Butan* frontier, and as they load goats and sheep with the merchandise, these feed themselves wherever they stop ; and, as great flocks are driven by two or three people, the transport is attended with little real cost to the *Marchas*. But the commerce of the present day is said to be a mere trifle in comparison with the traffic of former times. The goats used for this business are of the breed of this country, migrate regularly twice a year, are short-legged, of a strong compact form and travel about 5 cos a day over the most rugged and difficult roads that can be imagined.

The principal articles of the food of the most wealthy consist in the morning of boiled rice and goats' flesh and at night of cakes made of wheat-flour beaten with water and seasoned with salt and clarified butter ; as also of curds and fresh milk of sheep and goats. But wheat-flour is scarcely ever tasted by the poor who live upon the coarsest and most common kinds of grain, and, when they can get it, eat flesh raw, as has been before observed. Wheat is not raised in this district, but grows to a good height near *Joshi-Math*. The following grains are raised here :

1st. Chua or Marcha ; resembling the Amaranthus Gangeticus or *Lal Sag* of the *Hindus* ; used here both fresh, and in its seed when reduced to flour.

2d. Manrua or Manrwe : Cynosurus Coracanus.

3d. Phaphei—This looks a little like *French* wheat.

4th. Coarse red rice.

5th. Ana Jau.—I have not seen this growing, but the grain unshelled looks like barley. Shelled, like a poor kind of wheat.

6th. Barley.

7th. Chani or Chena. Panicum Miliaceum.

8th. Cangne. Panicum Italicum.

9th. Jangora.

Slaves are much employed and are bought from the *Gorkhiahs*. In the evening my fakir harcarah, with a real fakir, arrived with intelligence that one of the women carriers who had followed the circuitous track I had taken on the 31st, being much fatigued, went to the river to drink and placed herself on a large stone, which slipping, caused her to fall into the water. The rapidity of the current was such as to hurry her out of her depth, and she was drowned. This matter affected me considerably. On inquiry I found she was without a family.

June 3d.—Leave *Malari* at 9 A.M. At 6165 paces, reach our encampment. The quantity of common and lemon thyme near water courses was very great, but none of it had been cropped by sheep ; I also saw basil, savory, mint and other potherbs, with sedums of several kinds ; and I likewise met with some gooseberry-bushes.

June 4th.—After breakfasting in a cave, at the foot of which runs a clear rill down a deep and broad rivulet half choked with a body of frozen snow, we left our ground at 7¼ A.M. After proceeding 5145 paces, arrive at the village of *Niti.* In the latter part of this day's march, I found my rate of breathing quickened beyond its natural standard in proportion to the difficulty of ascent, and was obliged frequently to stop, in order that the action of the heart might become less violent. My companion has been aware of occasional oppression in breathing for the last three days but I did not experience any till this day. The very wretched appearance of the 14 or 16 houses, which compose the town, gives no favourable expectation of the supplies we should here meet with.

June 5th.—The situation of *Niti* is in itself pretty enough, being at the foot of a small sweep of hills which defend it from the N. and W. A gorge, between the Western hills and those to the South, gave entrance to the *Niti* river and the valley is shut up, about a mile to the E., by an ascent covered with birch trees and leading to many gorges and ridges of a high mountain topped with snow. Down the side of the mountain, immediately in face of the town and extending from top to bottom, winds the track of a recent avalanche looking like a new made turnpike road. In front of the town, and between it and the river, are a few flats which descend by steps and have lately been ploughed. The town, following the line of the base of the rocks, was originally built in a crescent, but many of the houses have been deserted and unroofed and now serve only as night stable for cattle.

We sent a message to the *Sehana**, importing that we should be glad to see him. The meeting took place at our tent and the *Sehana* whose name was Arjun, began by stating that this was a road which pilgrims to *Mansarowar* seldom came that we were armed ; that we had many people ; that report said we were either *Gorkhalis* or *Firingis*, come with designs inimical to the *Undes*, and that measures had been taken accordingly. We endeavoured to remove these unfavourable impressions, and after much conversation the old man seemed satisfied. We wrote a letter in *Hindustani* to the *Deba*, informing him that for pious and humane purposes, we wished to visit the lake of *Mansarowar*, that for defraying our expenses we had brought certain articles from our country for sale ; that we had for our own defence certain arms which we were willing to leave in his keeping during our stay in the *Undes*. On urging to the *Sehana* the necessity of our speedy departure, he observed that the snow was not yet sufficiently melted ; that the communication was never attempted before the *Sancrant*, or entering of the sun into the next sign and that this would happen in fifteen days ; when they would accompany us, in case the answer of the *Deba* should be favourable to our intentions. The argument of the road not being open was falsified by the appearance of the *Unias* but it was thought best to wait an answer from the *Deba*.

From the 5th to the 9th, the thermometer at sun-rise has

---

*The Headman of a village is called Shana, or Sehana, Seyana.

been generally at 46°, but in the middle of the day about 72°. The nights have commonly been clear and serene, but there have been a few slight showers of rain in two of them. About nine it becomes pleasantly warm ; at noon it is sultry ; about three the heat generally and suddenly subsides and the tops of the highest mountains are enveloped in clouds, which deposit their contents on them in the form of snow, and in very gentle showers of rain in the valley of *Niti*. The changes in the temperature of the atmosphere are very sudden and severe.*

---

* On a subsequent day Mr. Moorcroft obseives *June 12th.* The temperature of the air varies much in the course of the day and night. At sun-rise, the thermometer is from 40° to 50° ; in the middle of the day from 70° to 80°. At eight in the morning the sun overtops the hills which surround the little valley of *Niti* and blazes with a fierceness of which we were the more sensible from the cold of the morning. About three the heat falls off most rapidly. I have never before experienced so sudden a transition from heat to cold, and contrariwise. At night I am only comfortably warm with almost all the bed clothes I can muster. At sun-rise a thick coarse woollen *Hindustani Chapkal* or wrapping gown, over shirt, cotton waistcoat, and double cotton coat, is only just sufficient to keep out the cold. At nine the outer coat must be thrown off; at ten it is desirable to get quit of the other; and at noon the rest of the garments are, to say the least, incommodious from the heat. The reverse of this progress becomes necessary from half past three till night. The frequent changes of the temperature produce colds and fevers both amongst the inhabitants and strangers : but, thought rather active in their symptoms they are neither dangerous nor of long continuance. Ordinarily from the morning till about three o'clock, there is an upper and under current in the atmosphere. The clouds are generally white during this time; move briskly towards the north, and change their forms with much vivacity. Their speed is commonly checked as they approach the most lofty mountains, to which they decline, and if they do not come so much within their influence as to burst upon them, they regain by degrees their former course. But about three the clouds become more murky, are stationary, envelope the summits of the mountains, and roll down their sides, discharging their contents in the form of snow upon the highest, and in light showers of rain upon the lower ones. The lower current is formed by the interruption given to the under strata of the higher current by the irregular form of the land beneath, and is almost continually varying in direction. During still nights the dew falls very heavily : but, when there is a little motion in the atmosphere, the humidity is suspended above the

In the morning the summits of the highest mountains are wholly concealed by the snow ; about noon the ridges between the ravines are cleared but it remains in the clefts and gorges ; and from three to the following morning the mountain has a new covering. This succesive deposition and melting go on during the warm months. But, in the cold weather, when the mountaineers are obliged to quit their habitations and leave them to be taken possession of by such wild animals as prefer them to taking an asylum in caverns and glens. The whole surface of the valleys as well as mountains, is richly covered with snow which in some parts melts under the influence of heat and rain, but in others remains continually. This mass of melted snow on the vast ranges of mountains forms the great rivers which proceed from them.

When we arrived, the *Niti* river, about ten yards broad and from two to four feet deep, sent down a rapid stream of greenish but clear water. The two following days were very hot : the stream was on the 3d, at least a foot deeper and considerably broader, and the water is clay-coloured and turbid. I have frequently observed that the water-mark early

---

valley and attracted by the hills. The stars are very brilliant, and the north star is beautifully resplendent. A bed of clear light-coloured air in the darkest night overhangs the summits of the peaks which are covered with snow. Once only lightning has been observed ; but, there has been no thunder during our stay. Does the great height of the mountains carry off the electricity of the atmosphere, before it can be accumulated in quantity sufficient to displace a body of air with the violence necessary to produce an explosion ? I regret that we have no means of measuring our actual height above the level of the sea All of us feel much inconvenience through it being necessary to breathe very frequently, even when going as slowly as possible upon an easy ascent. We anticipate great fatigue from this cause on scaling the stupendous heights over which the road lies. The natives recommend a small quantity of coarse sugar to be eaten whilst we are mounting, and speak highly of the power of the kind of spar found near the snow reduced to powder and mixed with water, in diminishing the distressingly quickened action of breathing. This spar they believe to be snow gradully melted and again condensed and crystalized by continual cold, and call it *Himgal* from *Him*, snow ; and *gal*, from *galana*, to melt.

in the morning upon the stones in the river was a foot and even eighteen inches above the level of the stream at that time of the day and that the river always rose considerably towards the evening. This is easily explained by the cold of the night produced by the snow on the mountains suspending the melting process, and of course interrupting the supply until the heat of the following day quickens it again. Such a surface of mountainous country, in such a state, along with the vast declivity of the beds of the rivers, will afford a more satisfactory explanation of the real sources of the *Ganges* than the deriving it from a lake which must have some continual source of supply itself.

The birch trees upon the sides of the mountains as well as the small rose-bushes, are just breaking into leaf; the furze is just coming into blossom. The natives have some barley of which a few blades appear and they are engaged in getting into the ground the *awa-jou*, *phaphar* and *chua*. This is, it is presumed, their spring and our rains must be their summer, as their harvest is cut before the middle of *September* when the people go in search of a milder climate.

This morning (the 9th) I saw a beautiful crop of rock crystal shooting out of an exposed layer of quartz which had formerly been a vein in a mass of very hard stone. These mountains which are primordial, would, if examined by an able and careful lithologist, throw great light upon the natural history of the mineral kingdom; for here, at almost every step, he might come in sight of the surfaces of rock which have never been altered by the hand of man but have alone been subject to the laws of composition and of destruction, induced by the operation of natural causes.

With the exception of grain of various kinds which is to be obtained at an exorbitant rate, little eatable is to be procured at *Niti*. The only animal food which we have had, has been two or three lean goats. There was no want of kids or lambs but the owners would only sell such as were ill or extremely old. This country at the present season gives no fruit. The inhabitants have no gardens and the only esculent vegetables, which we could find, were the *Bathua* (Chenopodium album), a small quantity of self-sown *phaphar* about three inches high, and some rhubarb, the leaves of which were only just springing from the ground, yet even in this early state of vegetating, the flowers were thrown out on the sides of short finger-like processes and yielded a sweet smell. The vital principle seems to be most rapidly called into action amongst the vegetables of this climate to compensate for the long period during which they remain in a torpid state. Our diet was certainly of a very frugal kind and would not have been considered luxurious even in the cell of an anchorite, but our beverage was water of so excellent a quality as to make up for the scantiness and uniformity of it. We had been promised by the Pandit that we should have an opportunity of seeing and probably of killing some *Barals*. The first part was verified for they made their appearance amongst the furze bushes, almost immediately above our heads and at the foot of the bare rocks, but never came within gun shot. Although we were told that the richer *Marchas* sometimes ate animal food, I believe that this occurs very seldom. They are much subject to fevers from derangement of the intestines, brought on from vegetable diet little seasoned, and several have the *Gegha* or *Goitre*.

June 13th.—This day two *Uniyas* arrived at *Niti* with a letter to the *Sihana*, which neither they nor he could decypher. However, a meeting was held upon the substance of the message which they brought, by the head persons of the principal villages in this neighbourhood. The letter was supposed to be a formal rejection of our desire to enter the country. This conclusion was drawn from the refusal of the *Deba* to accept our present and from the verbal notification to us of the decease of the *Lama*, and of large bodies of troops having been detached to all the passes leading from the mountains into the *Undes*, to prevent the entrance of any white people or persons wearing white clothes, into the country until after the election of another *Lama*. This message was, of course, very disagreeable to us ; however, we were resolved not to return without having made every effort in our power to succeed in our orginal project. The people of *Niti* confessed that they were alarmed at the reports which had been circulated respecting us, previously to our arrival : but, that on seeing more of us, they had sent a *Funia* or *Vakil* to the *Deba* of *Daba*, stating that they believed we were men of character really intending to go to *Mansarowar*, having merchandise to dispose of and not harbouring any evil design against the general welfare of the country. We knew that the *Vakil* had been dispatched two days subsequently to the departure of the first two *Uniyas*, but we placed little dependence upon the impression he would make. The commencement of his mission certainly took off much from the accustomed dignity of his post ; for, in attempting to ride upon a bullock, he with difficulty mounted, in consequence of being very drunk and fell off four times before he was able to reach the top of the mountain.

June 16th.—Another great meeting took place. The *Uniyas* insisted upon our not being permitted to pass ; and the *Seyanas* of *Niti* and *Gomasale*, Arjun and Gujar Mall were decidedly against us, especially the latter. Hardeb was sent back with money to the brother cf Nathu, a relation of Ramkishen, *Seyana* of *Malari*, who had shewn an inclination to assist us to bring bullocks immediately, that we might attempt proceeding by the road of *Lieulang* and we laid in ten days' provision for all our men in order that we might not lose any time at *Malari* in collecting it. Ramkishen acquainted us with the opinion of the council, said he would hasten all our operations at *Malari* ; and Hardeb was ordered to bring a *Jowari* (who had made an offer to us of conducting us in three days from *Malari* into the *Undes*) with promises of safe conduct to *Niti* and back, and of reward for his services. Hopes were entertained, that in some way we should still succeed by persuasive means with the people of *Niti*. However, we thought it right to take all such measures, as might appear likely to gain our point without loss of time.

Another meeting was appointed two days afterwards at *Gomsale*. In the course of this morning two persons had come from *Negi* Bhawani Sena, with a letter requesting the loan of one hundred and one rupees, to be repaid either in carriage of articles, in provision or in specie with interest at 2 per cent per mensem, and a bond for the amount, along with a statement of the prices at which we should receive provisions. He said that he understood we were delayed and advised our getting on quickly.

In the evening Amar Singh, the son of the *Seyana* Arjun, declared to the Pandit that, if we would place confidence in him, he would take our baggage to the frontier, would make an arrangement with the *Deba* by becoming surety for us and would go with us to *Mansarowar*, after which he would settle in *Jowar*, as he was apprehensive that the *Negi* would have recourse to some harsh measures with him, in consequence of his quarrelling with Jowahar Singh and causing his servant to be beaten. He said if the council at *Gomsale* were friendly, it would be well ; if not, he had five bullocks and would see what was to be done in respect to the further number required. His father was convinced that we were persons to be depended upon and was privy to the transaction. As is seemed on many accounts perferable to take the *Daba* road, the old Pandit on our part went to the father and son in the night to take their oaths for the proformance of their covenant. This next day Hardeb returned with an account of Nathu's brother having repented of his declaration, of Ramkishen's slackness, and of his not being able to purchase any bullocks although at double their value. It has been agitated whether the *Seyanas* altogether, shall become sureties for us, but as yet this motion has been negatived. Once it was proposed that we should leave our property at *Niti* and go on with cloths and provision alone. This was, of course, rejected by us as ridiculous. It was then submitted, whether we would allow them to take it and sell it whilst we should stay for the proceeds. This was rejected likewise and declared our determination to march alone if they would not assist us with cattle.

The *Funia* arrived on the 19th, and by him it appeared clearly that it depended soley upon the people of this country to give us an introduction, for the *Deba* said he hoped the *Niti Marchas* would not give us carriage, observing "if they have not conveyance for their baggage and provision, they cannot come, but if provided with carriage, as there are no troops hereabouts, there is no method of preventing their entry into the country". The *Funia* also hinted that a moderate present to the *Deba* would overcome all difficulties.

June 22nd. Amer Singh says that we shall certainly break ground tomorrow, but as yet we see no preparation, save amongst ovrselves.

June 23rd.—Still difficulties are started against our proceeding, until there shall be a general consent of the heads of villages to enter into a security for our good conduct with the *Deba* of *Daba.* We have had no small degree of difficulty in causing Arjun to fix terms for the hire of his cattle. At length we have fixed that each bullock shall carry the accustomed loads of two men and not exceed five rupees. Understanding that all the people concerned in our affairs were drinking at Arjun's house, we made a bottle of brandy into a kind of punch, well sweetened, and sent it, in hopes that its influence might be beneficial to our cause ; in the opinion of the party it had only the fault of being too limited in quality.

June 24th.—We were disturbed during last night by the shoutings of men and almost continual barking of dogs. Two large bears had broken into a sheep-and-goat-pen and carried off one of the goats.

We rose at a very early hour to prepare our baggage for loading, as nine bullocks had been brought to *Niti* the night before, but after being ready for two hours without Amer Singh or any of his people coming, we sent word that we wished to proceed. This brought old Arjun who desired us to delay our journey three days longer, when every things should be ready. His reasoning was very unsatisfactory, and we urged him to fulfil his contract. In consequence of our remonstrances, he promised that we shculd being our march today even if Gujar would not consent, although he was particularly anxious to obtain his concurrence to the measure. After waiting another hour, Gujar made his appearance and made many objections to our journey. He Gujar, received a present of ten rupees, but I had reason to believe that he expected more. Arjun had five and we had friends amongst the women, in consequence of medicines given to them, as also of silver rings and other trifles which I had distributed. After a delay of two hours more we took our leave of *Niti* ; my companion and myself then mounted on a *chounr* bullock*. We were told that the first march was to reach *Gutang*, a place five cos distant, where we were to halt two days. This compromise we were really happy to make, for it was evident that it was the intention of the people to detain us at *Niti* as long as possible, for objects of their own.

Left *Niti* at 11.20. After travelling a mile, the people would not go any further, saying they were not prepared to proceed to *Gutang*, and that they would be with us the following day. They wished to solemnize the anniversary of the death of one of the villagers which happened by accident twelve months ago and their march to *Buthant* (*Bootan*) at the same time and notwithstanding their promise, it was understood that they would take up two days in this festival.

Our encampment was on the slope of a hill, situated between the foot of high mouldering mountains and the river *Dauli*, not farther than a mile in direct distance from *Niti*. However, we had made a start and were in a better posture for defence, in case of any attack being made upon us, than at *Niti*, for in front of us there was a deep rivulet ; on our right, looking towards *Niti* whence only we had anything to apprehend, was the river *Dauli* and, on the left flank, mountains which could not be turned without immense difficulty.

June 25th —Rain fell during the night and, as the cattle had been turned loose to graze the preceeding day, I resolved to go towards the rocks. We had heard the call of birds, which we took to be pheasants. I was three hours in reaching the base of the line of rocks which seemed not quite three miles from our encampment and though I climbed as slowly as possible, I was obliged to stop ever five or six paces to take breath and the person who accompanied me were affected in the same manner. In respect to game my search was unsuccessful, but I met with many plants ; amongst others were two kinds

*The Yak of Tartary. Bos grunniens.

of rhubarb. One I took for the Rheum palmatum the other was much smaller. I cut up the roots of many large plants. The leaves in several instances sprung from a little sound bark which surrounded a large portion that was rotten. Those which were hard, were detached from the sound part of the bark near the surface of the ground, but these shrunk much in drying and had but little of the rhubarb taste, colour or smell, whilst the sound fragments of the root of the preceding year were marbled like the cut surface of a nutmeg : some were yellow, and had the peculiar qualities of the rhubarb, with a very large proportion of a bright colouring matter which stained the finger of a gold tint, but I presume that the best time for taking up the roots is in *September*. If the quality of this root should be found to equal that of the *Levant*, the quantity procurable here at an easy rate would be very great.

We have learnt that the carousals of last night were kept up so long as to have prevented the partakers from undertaking any kind of business.

June 26th.—Early this morning I went up the mountains. The ascent was very laborious from the great difficulty of breathing which we all experienced yesterday, out of five people, two only were able to go as far as I did ; today only one out of four could keep company with me and he requested me to return, as the cold made him suffer much. The wind blew fresh up the mountain in the line of direction which I was taking, but I found that I could not take above five or six steps straight forwards without stopping to take breath. I, therefore, ascended by zigzags of eight or ten paces, which afforded the opportunity of having a side wind in each oblique line. After a toilsome ascent of five hours, I reached a small flat of table land which, if alone, would have been considered, as of great height ; but was of minor importance in the presence of rocks of such stupendous loftiness, as those which hid their summits in the clouds. This was covered with a dark green carpet formed by a short narrow-leaved grass of a springy nature and enamelled with small blue polyanthuses in tufts, with anemones and ranunculuses, but not with any of remarkable brilliancy of colour ; after collecting all the varieties within my reach, I prolonged my march, following the track of a *chounr* bullock up the hill. I was obliged to continue my oblique march but, on turning my back to the wind, felt a sudden fulness in my head accompanied by giddiness and fearing apoplexy, I threw myself on the ground with precipitation. After a short time the gasping for breath became less frequent, the action of the head was less violent, and I quitted the turf ; but although I walked as leisurely as possible, I was twice again attacked with the same symptoms, and thought it most prudent to desist asccending any higher. The imperious necessity for stopping to breathe every four or five steps was only felt whilst ascending ; when the impetuous action of the heart was reduced by remaining quiet in one place, no difficully in breathing was perceived nor was it felt in descending, even in a run, where this was practicable, but several times at our encampment, when about to fall asleep, I have been interrupted by the same sensation. Although not particularly aware of any remarkable degree of heat or of cold, yet I found my hands, neck and face very red and the skin sore, and blood had burst from my lips : a circumstance which I do not recollect to have happened to me before.

June 27th.-Hearing nothing from the *Niti* people, a messenger was dispatched to learn the cause of their not coming. He went off about ten in the morning and said that he found all the inhabitants fast asleep from the effects of intoxication. Men, women and children were lying in one promiscuous heap upon the floor, with difficulty he awoke two people who stated that Arjun would be with us in the evening and that we should assuredly march the following morning. They had killed several goats and burnt the entrails, and some other parts on an altar, but had feasted on the remainder. When a person dies, it is customary to invite all the relations and friends of the deceased to a supper and dance. The night is spent in feasting and drinking at the expense of the property of the deceased ; and not unfrequently, the revelry is attended with bloodshed, as was the case last night, three persons having been wounded with swords.

In the evening Arjun came and promised that we should

start in the morning ; but desired to have a bond of indemnity against any mischief that might be done by any of our party in *Undes*. This was complied with, we promising to pay five times the amount of any damage done.

June 28th.—Thermometer 51½, depart at 7 A.M. At 3605 paces cross melting snow. At 5917 came to our halting ground on the bank of the river. This is called *Gutanp nacli*. Here we found the goats and sheep belonging to the *Marchas* of *Ghomsali Pharkia* and *Niti*, who are going to *Bootan* with grain. Two P.M, thermometer in tent 74°. In the evening Amer Sing and Gujar's son arrived. Rain continued great part of the night.

June 29th.—Thermometer 50°, morning cloudy and rainy. Leave our ground at six A.M. At 1560 paces the *Dauli* is joined by the *Hiwangal* which rises from the *Nar-Narayan* mountain of *Bhadra Nath*, and is a considerable stream. The joint stream is about twenty-five yards broad. Proceed over blocks of stone along the left bank of the *Dauli*, which hurries down its bed a great body of snow water. At 2370 paces a bed of snow forms an arch, under which the river runs ; this bed was about forty yards long and ten thick. At 2680 paces arrive at another, over the edge of which we proceed. At 3109 paces reach another, which like the former passes over the river. At 3580 paces cross on a *Sankho* to the right bank ; river about sixteen feet broad but rapid ; ascend a difficult hill. At 4630 paces reach its summit. This is the road for the early part of the season ; at a later period the best road is along the right bank of the river. The stream is about 700 feet below the top of the ascent just mentioned. At 7350 paces cross a broad water-course called *Patarpani*, proceeding from the mountains and carrying a considerable body of water, due E. into the *Dauli* about a mile distant. On the other side of the river another water-course coming from the E. by S. empties itself into the great stream.

We had been obliged to comply with the extravagant terms of the *Niti* people at the rate of fourteen *Timashas** for every

---

* The silver coin of Srinagar and Latakh ; which should wigh, as the name imports, three mashas, the fourth part of a rupee : but the present currency has been much debased.

load and a bullock was rated at two loads, that is twenty-five *Timashas* ; we wished that there should be a stated weight but this they would not comply with and a cow was entered as being equal to a bullock. This proved unused to carry borthens, as she three times threw off her load ; at length disengaging herself from what she carried, she ran away and I was obliged to dismount and put her load on my bullock. The *Niti* people had proposed to carry flour for us to *Daba* at a moderate price on goats but we could not bring them to specific terms before we started, and were obliged to keep this matter open, notwithstanding this renders us still more liable to be imposed upon. Today they insisted that three goats were equal to the hire of one man and although this rate is higher than the absolute value of the goats, we were obliged to submit to the imposition. At *Niti* our *Bareli* rupees were current in payment for five *Timashas* ; at this place the carriers will only consider them equal to four ; this circumstance explains one reason of the dely in settling the rate of hire.

June 30th.—Thermometer 46 at sun-rise. It has rained great part of the night and the summits of the neighbouring mountains are sprinkled with snow. Yesterday the first part of our march was through a narrow gulley giving course to the *Dauli*, the bed of which was formed by the union of the base of mountains of great height. Those which were principally composed of sand-stone, had their feet concealed by a large slope of sand and small pieces of stone, and their summits were ragged and rapidly breaking down. Of this description for the most part were those on the left bank of the river and their craggy irregular tops were far removed from the channel. Those of the right bank were principally of granite of a green colour, where washed with the water, and blue, blackish and brown above. The face of these, though by far more perpendicular than the other, and in most instances almost entirely so, shewed manifest signs of the destroying power of the weather. Some of the blocks of stone, which lay in the channel of the river, were of a kind of pudding stone, the insulated pebbles being of a raddish or bluish colour and the cementing material of green granite ; were these masses in situations where they could be worked, they would furnish most beautiful slabs, as their union is most intimate and the friction of the water alone has given to many of them thc smoothest surface imaginable. At the union of the *Dauli* with the *Hiwangal*, we took leave of trees; the last we saw being birch and small firs on the right bank of the *Dauli*, just after the other stream had fallen into it. The character of the mountains before and on each side of the slope, on which we were encamped last night, is of a different nature; though bold in their forms, their outline is rounder, less abrupt and the line of their summits more continued and agreeable.

I awoke at a very early hour and was immediately seized with difficulty of breathing and great oppression about the heart, which was removed for a few seconds by sighing deeply. When on the point of falling asleep, the sense of suffocation came on, and the sighing became very frequent and distressing; however, as the air became a little warmer, this affection somewhat subsided. Several of the people are suffering from headaches, colds, and affections of the intestimes, apparently attributable to the great and sudden changes in the state of the air as in the middle of the day, the thermometer often stood 30° higher than in the morning.

March at six. At 3021 paces, desert the *Dauli*, within two cos from its source at the foot of a mountain called the *Gauganoli*. At 5360 paces, commence ascending the *Ghati* or pass which separates *Hindustan* from *Undes*. Ascent very steep and difficult. We rode upon our bullocks the whole of the ascent which was a mile and three quarters. At 7470 paces reach the summit where we find a heap of stones, on which is a pole with pieces of rag attached to it, and as it is customary for every caravan or even for a single traveller to add his mite, we ordered a bit of cloth to be suspended in our name. This custom is supposed to entail the accomplishment of the objects of the journey to every one who observes it. We passed over an extensive plain thickly covered with large stones, upon which the bullocks tread with extraordinary firmness. This plain is bounded on every side with mountains; those behind are covered with snow without any mark of vegetation; those before are equally bare, but without snow. Distance this day about five miles and a half.

The first ascent was very steep, but not so difficult as the second, which is called the *Niti Ghati* or pass. Here our conductor, Amer Singh, had some fears that our progress might be impeded by some guards from *Daba*, and whilst ascending, called to the Pandit, who had got the start of him, to examine whether there were any watchmen on the summit. He appeared not a little gratified on learning that there were not any. The height of this pass is so great and long, that a very small body of resolute men on the top might defend it almost against a large army, merely by rolling down stones.

We found the sun hot about eleven, when we began to climb; but it was stated that about three it became so cold that it would be scarcely possible to support it ; however, I conceive this to be an exaggeration. In some parts of the stony plain, the snow lay in masses, over which the bullocks trod without hesitation ; and in others, it was melting. Part of this gently ran over the surface into ravines, and part soaked into the ground, and probably broke out in springs at distant places. Between the *Niti Ghati* and the northern face of a hill adjoining a stream called the *Jandu*, there was not the smallest trace of vegetation. The distance were about one half cos; but just on the brow of the hill declining to the river, were some bushes of furze and green mounds formed by a kind of moss, which is remarkably close and firm. The stony plain was of great breadth, and was intersected by deep and broad ravines, which took off the melting snows. These ravines all ran towards the North and East, and are the sources of various streams, which joining in their course, give rise to the *Setlij*. The last range of hills had been represented as not so high as many in *Garwal*. However, from the view which I have had of them, it appears to me that they are higher ; and the general difficulty of breathing experienced by us in passing them comes in confirmation of this opinion.

We encamped on some flat ground on the bank of the *Jandu*, a river which receives the *Sheku*, and another branch from the northern face of the great *Himalaya* range. It was extremely hot when we arrived ; and as there was no natural shelter, I laid myself on the ground under a thick blanket. Though oppressed with desire for sleep, I found it impossible to indulge the inclination, in consequence of oppression in breathing, the moment I was dropping asleep ; and deep sighing only proved a temporary relief. At three o'clock the wind became very violent, but abated in the morning a little before sunrise. Two *Uniyas*, going to *Niti* with salt, here met Amer Singh, and started, as he said many objections to our proceeding. He thought it prudent, that they should return with us, lest they might spread some report that might be prejudicial to us.

3

JOURNEY TO LAKE MANSAROVAR : JULY 1ST TO JULY 31ST

July 1st.—Thermometer at sun-rise 41° ; match at 5.35 A.M. At 3205 paces reach the summit where there is a heap of stones. Here we found the two *Uniyas*, one of whom was busied in lighting a fire, into which the other threw some incense, which he had previously bruised on a stone. He then leisurely walked round the pile of stones in the midst of which was a statue having piece of cloth tied to it and, whilst walking, uttered a long prayer. To the East was the sacred mountain near the lake of *Mansarovar*, tipped with snow and called *Cailas* or *Mahadeo ka Ling*. Turning his face towards this mountain, and after raising his hands with the palms joined above his head, then touching his forehead, he suddenly placed them on the ground, and going on his knees, pressed his forehead to the ground. This raising of the hands, and prostration of the body and head, was repeated seven times ; the other *Uniya*, less devout perhaps, contented himself with three salutations and a short prayer.

---

1. There are two mountains of this latter name : one near *Gangotri*, the other at *Cailas*.

Came to a large plain divided into several portions by broad ravines, and having several broad but not high hills on it. The only marks of vegetation upon it are low bushes of the furze, which may be called Tatarian, and small mounds of the compact moss before mentioned, with here and there a small tuft of a thin silky grass just springing up. Patches of snow still upon the ground, and splashes of water in which the feet sunk considerably. Although I give our *Niti* friends credit for detaining us as long as possible, I nevertheless think we should have found some difficulty in passing these plains ten days ago, from their then swampy state. At 5400 paces, leave some snow in a hollow close to the left. At 5840 paces, come to another heap of stones, and descend rapidly along a ridge between a water course, now dry, to the right, and one to the left, having a stream running down its bed. At 6000 paces descend. At 6965 paces, encamp on the left bank of the *Chastu* river, the source of which bears S. 70 W. and springs from the northern base of the great *Himalaya* ridge. The bed of the *Chagla* river is about the sixth of a mile broad, pebbly and fleet, with several small but rapid currents running down it. The rivers to the South of the great *Himalaya* ridge are narrow, from the sides of the hills being very steep and their bases forming a narrow angle with little valley. Those which rise on the northern base of the same ridge have broad flat channels, the water draining into them more slowly from the table-land and the more gradual and gentle slopes of the hills.

A hunter, whom we have long employed unsuccessfully, this evening brought in a female *Baral*[2]. It was about the height of a hog deer, (Cervus porcinus) with its legs and feet much like the sheep, and some similarity in the head, but the ears were thinner and narrower. It had eight teeth and two horns which curved lightly backwards. Its hair was very hard, and on the neck close to the skin grew some fine wool. Its general colour was ash or grey, but it had its shins and tail darker than the rest, and under the belly it was nearly white. It had four stomachs and a gall-bladder ; a vesicular taenia

---

2. Seems to be Ovis Ammon, C.

was in the mesentery, but I broke it in endeavouring to extract it. Were it not fanciful to suppose a chain in the works of nature, I should say that this animal was the link between the deer and the sheep.

In crossing the plains I have seen no insects save a few small yellow butterflies ; no reptiles but a little active lizard of a dun tint ; no game, and no birds save the red *Tuti*, larks and linnets : but at our encampment there were ravens of a large size with a loud caw, an immensely large eagle on the wing, and a blue pigeon with lighter plumage than that common in *Hindustan.* I conceive that no trip would be more instructive to the physiological Botanist than one across the mountains which separate *Hindustan* from *Tatary*, as plants of the same kind vary in their size, tints and strength, according to the difference of their situations. Sometime I thought that I was mistaken, but having seen the habitudes of many flowers differ extraordinarily in different places, and as the difference between those on the summits of gigantic mountains, and at the bottom of profound glens, was presented very frequently to my eye with intermediate shades in intermediate places, as to elevation within a short space, I was enabled to recognise their identity of family, after a little time, without difficulty. At sun-set high wind arose. Thermometer 54°.

July 2nd.—Thermometer 5, A.M. 44° ; wind subsided during the night. The general direction of the rivers which we now meet with is E. by N., although they rise from S.70 W. As the cattle had strayed, we were delayed until half past eight. At 5168 paces the mountain, along which we have come this morning, ends parallel to the left one. At 6845 paces arrive at our encamping ground, which is bad, as there is only one small spring, from which the water is taken by a small ladle as fast as the hole fills, and this is very slowly. Here we found a square tent of black blankets pitched with four poles at the corner and belonging to some *Uniyas* who had come from *Daba* to graze their goats. As the water was not in sufficient quantity for the supply of the *Uniyas* and the *Niti* people, another well was dug, which gave what was required for cooking ; but that for drinking was brought nearly three cos. An *Uniya* woman, wife to one of the goatherds, very good-naturedly filled the water-vessels of those persons who came to the little well, and did not take up her own part till the different candidates for water received the quantity which they asked for. She had rather a pleasing countenance, was of middle stature, and about thirtyfive years old. There was much of curiosity in her looks at seeing us, but nothing of fear or impertinence. Her dress was woollen, and of the same form with that of the men. Her boots were likewise woollen, and much diversified by patches of various hues. Her hair, which was of a deep black, was plaited in tresses from the forehead down to below her waist, where the plaits to the number of fifty, after each being terminated by a cowrie shell were assembled in a band of leather which was tipped with a tassel of red worsted thread : her head-lappet, if I may so name it, was of leather, and extended from the forehead down the back to the waist, but in the latter part gradually ended in a point. At the forehead it was bordered with silver, and from this rim hung seven rows of coral beads, each row consisting of five, which were terminated by seven silver *Timashas* that played upon the forehead. The crown of the lappet was studded with small pearls distributed in seven rows, and the lower parts was decorated with green stones something like turquoises, but marbled, with coral beads, and many bands of silver, and of a yellow metal, probably gold, about a finger's breadth. A stiff band of leather something like a soldier's collar was placed loosely round her neck, and ornamented with five rows of coral beads. The collar was secured with a button and clasp of silver. In her left ear was a coral bead set in silver, and in her right were two smaller beads in the same material. On her right thumb she wore a square gold ring with characters engraved on the table.

On quitting the spring in the way to our encampments, we saw some of the *Bampo Marchas* sitting by their loads, with a dead sheep lying on the ground in its fleece, but having the entrails taken out ; on a dish lay some of the intestines cut in lengths like black puddings, and I was led by this to inquire what they were and how made ; and from the intimation which I received, was a little surprised to find the borderers of *Bootan*, well acquainted with the art of making black puddings. The carcass of the sheep was afterwards, I understood, roasted whole, by being frequently turned in a fire of furze roots.

This day we were treated with some chops from our *Baral,* and we found the flesh juicy, tender and high flavoured. There was a *Bootan* priest sitting with some sheepherds from the neighbourhood, cheapening small wooden bowls turned out of knots of horse chesnut. They are very durable, the knotty structure preventing them from either breaking or warping. In the evening there were some peals of distant thunder and an appearance of much rain ; however we escaped with a few drops, the mass being attracted by the hills to the north. The *Uniyas* had dogs with their flocks, which were fierce and much disposed to attack strangers.

July 3d.—Thermometer at 5,—58°. Marched at 5,—10, as our conductors were anxious to reach *Daba* at an early hour, Road leading over a dry gravelly plain, much cracked and with little vegetation, except here and there some low bushes of furze, small tufts of a silky grass springing out of this cleft, and a woolly plant like that commonly called "everlasting," perhaps a kind of dittany. A snowy peak in front. The road lies over a plain of great length, but not of above seven cos in beadth and consisting of many levels or steps broken by deep ravines, the edges of some of which are as level as if executed by art. On the south, the plain is bounded by the last *Himalaya* ridge, just tipped with snow in stripes like foot-paths, extending along the windings of the ridges : on the north, by the *Cailas* mountains, the summit of which are marked more distinctly with snow, and the bases of which descend to the level of the plain by easy slopes and diminishing swells, forming a succession of steps separated from each other in the length of the plain by breast-works of broken ground. Behind, the mountains seem to meet in an angle near *Mahadeva ka Ling* ; but the plain seems to expand before us till it is shut in by stupendous mountains, whose sides, as well as craggy summits, are apparently very thickly covered with snow. To the left, or rather to the S.W., are the mountains of *Baschar.* At the distance of about two miles, a little to the W. of N. is a most extraordinary face of broken ground. This represents pyramids, in some places joining their tops but separate at their bases ; in others, separate at their tops but clusted at their foundations : buttresses of various proportions and forms ; and no unapt resemblances to ruined castles and fortifications in piles above each other.

The town of *Daba* is perched upon the top of a rock, which juts out towards the river with an irregular declivity, and is surmounted by the highest eminence in the whole line which defends it from the N.W. At 5306 paces the river close below and a few cultivated fields, which are the first we have seen in this country : encamp near a rivulet in the town.

It was considered proper that Amer Singh should announce our arrival to the *Deba*, and inquire when we might wait upon him. It seems that there are three personages of importance here, the *Lama*, the *Wazir* and the *Deba*, who is properly the head zemindar. The *Wazir* was absent on business towards *Mansarovar*, and his son officiated for him. Amer Singh reported, that the *Deba* and *Wazir's* son were very angry with him for having afforded us carriage, as without this assistance we could not have come on ; and he had more reason to be displeased, as he had sent two messengers to forbid our entering *Undes*. Amer Singh made excuse ; saying they had delayed from time to time furnishing bullocks under the expectation of our being wearied and giving up the idea of proceeding ; but that, so far from this producing the effect which he expected we threatened to make him advance not only the expense of our stay at *Niti*, which was considerable from the number of people we had with us, but also to pay the charges of the whole of a journey, which, by his not forwarding us, was likely to end in disappointment. But the *Deba* still remained displeased.

In the evening there was a consultation betwixt the *Wazir's* son, the *Deba* and the *Lama*, at which were present Amer Singh, the old pundit, a sircar and a *Jouar* man. It was stated by the *Deba's* people that it was necessary to report the matter to the military chief, who resided at the court of *Gortope*, a place about two days' journey distant, and who exercised a general governing power over the country.

July 4th.—Thermometer 54°. Amer Singh sent word, that the council was ready to receive our visit ; and we set out towards the government house, which was about a hundred yards distant, accompanied by a few servants. The house on the outside was not of a very imposing aspect, though built of stone. Over the door a large dog was tied, which eyed us with attention, but did not attempt to molest us. We passed through several passages and small anti-chambers full of people, into a low room of about 18 feet square in the middle of which was a small carpet for us to sit on. Immediately in front of us on a ledge raised about a foot, sat two young men, one of whom was represented as the *Wazir's* son, and the other as the *Deba*, each upon their cushions ; on their right, and forming the upper end of another line of persons extending from one side of the room to the other, the *Lama* was seated upon a leathern cushion, next to him a priest, and then an interpreter ; the *Seyanas* of *Niti* formed an opposite line ; and we were seated in the centre of a square of people, who, if not very clean, were at least orderly and respectful in their behaviour. The young men were large in their persons, the *Wazir's* son particularly so, and about twentyfive years of age ; the *Deba* was somewhat older ; in the features of both, the *Tatar* character was observable, though not in any very great degree. The *Lama* was about sixty, with a shaven head, dark complexion, serious and wrinkled countenance, and features of a common cast. The priest beside him was still darker, more ugly, and more greasy in his clothes, reclining partly on the floor, and partly on the ledge on the upper part of the room ; near to the *Deba* was a young woman of pleasing face, wife to the *Deba*, and daughter to the *Wazir*, with a pretty child in her arms, and the left returning line from the *Deba* was begun by a writer of dark countenance. The *Wazir's* son was dressed in a large loose coat or gown of woollen stuff, striped blue, yellow, green, and red, alternately about a finger's breadth, and said to be manufactured at *Guinnak*, the capital of *Chinese Tatary*. His hair was collected into one large plait which hung down his back, and he had no beard. The *Deba* had on a dark green woollen gown, and his hair was plaited in the like manner. His beard was plucked out, but he had reserved a thin mustachio on the upper lip ; both the *Wazir's* son and the *Deba*, wore broad rings on the right thumb. Their ostensible use was for defending the thumb in drawing the string of the bow ; but it served very conveniently also for trimming their tobacco-pipes, which lay in readiness beside them. These were about eighteen inches long, in the form of the *English* pipe, but made of iron, decorated with embossed work and a rim of gold, and a circle of the same metal at the union of the bowl with the stem. A small japanned table was before each, and on them were implements for writing with two round wooden boxes japanned, and a large red and white china tea-up. The *Lama* had before him also a japanned long and low stand, upon which was a round box. When we entered the room, the *Deba* was correcting a letter, which he had written to the commander of *Gortope*, and which he read over, desiring Amer Singh to explain the substance of it to us. He read with a distinct articulation, with occasional pauses. The language was soft ; and the substance, as far as we could collect it, was as follows. That Amer Singh, and other *Seyanas*, had brought along with them two *Mahants*, and twentyfive followers, who were desirous of proceeding on a pilgrimage to *Mansarovar* ; that the first representation of their being *Gorkhalis* or *Firingis*, was a mistake : and that the arms which they had with them, were only sufficient for their protection during solong and hazardous a journey as that which they had undertaken. That the *Seyanas* had entered into an engagement that these were real *Gosains*, who brought merchandise to defray their way expenses, and that they would be responsible both in their persons and property, that they should demean themselves peaceably and properly whilst they should remain in the country, paying for every thing they might require, and taking nothing by force ; and as they had been put to much unnecessary expense by their being delayed at *Niti*, the *Deba* trusted that the chief would give orders for their being allowed to proceed without delay. The *Deba* caused also a written agreement to be drawn out on the part of Amer Singh, binding himself to the truth of the above deposition in the name of the several *Seyanas*, and to which he affixed his seal. The letter was forwarded to the chief of *Gortope*, after the consent of the *Lama* had been received.

It was stated that the *Lama* had never before left his college on matters of business ; and we were to consider this as a great compliment paid to us. Between the *Lama* and the *Wazir's* son was an empty place which was supposed ordinarily to be filled by the *Wazir* ; and before this was laid down our present at our first coming into the chamber : inquiries were made whether we would drink tea or eat parched meal, which we declined on the score of having just risen from our repast, but which we could not accept in our character of *Hindus*, these people having no caste ; a large brass dish, half filled with butter and wheat-flour, was placed before us as some return for our present and we took our leave.

Yesterday a person came to us from the *Deba* to inquire after our health. He looked about my small tent with much curiosity, and observed that my friend's half-boots were like those of a *Feringi.* I had taken the precaution of having my *English* shoes furnished with long turn-up toes and tags at the heels, and this not being done to the others, excited his suspicion. The redness of my face, which, from being exposed to a hot sun and cold wind was almost wholly deprived of skin, particularly attracted his attention. The explanation given was, that, before this pilgrimage I had been but little exposed to the sun which had produced the effect which he saw. The same inquiry was made by a very black priest who came on the part of the *Lama,* and who said that if such was the influence of climate ; he supposed he should become white, if he were to go to the country I came from ; in about two hours after our visit was paid, the *Wazir's* son, the *Deba,* the interpreter, the *Deba,* wife and sister came to look at our finery, and admired several things, but found all our articles vastly too dear ; and I think in general they were right ; for we had affixed prices in some measure to make up for the expenses to which we had been subjected by imposition and delay. The *Deba's* wife fell in love with a ring which she actually asked for, and of course obtained. Five "children of a larger growth," who were extremely inquisitive, were desirous of knowing the contents of a bundle of my clothes ; they were made in the *Hindu* fashion. The *Deba* was anxious to see our guns ; but, from his mode of handling them, it was clear that he knew little of the use of fire-arms. We offered our guests tea, which they refused, but they partook of some sweet biscuits, gingerbread, and sugar-candy. After a stay of an hour, they left us, apparently satisfied with the reception which they had experienced.

July 5th.—Thermometer at sun-rise 48°. The town of Deba is situated partly upon irregular eminences, forming the side of a flat ravine descending rapidly to the river *Tiltil*, and in the bed of the ravine itself. Its situation, construction, and appearance, are altogether unlike any thing which I have ever seen before. The ravine, or bay, is surrounded by heights consisting of strata of indurated clay and thick beds of gravel. Some of these heights are above three hundred feet in elevation, others are less. They are broken into masses of various shape by the torrents of snow-water which fall down their sides. Some are like large buttresses with pointed tops ; and others, though of greater height, are surmounted by flat spaces. Their sides are full of excavations, to some of which are wooden doors; and others are merely caverns ; of these, some serve as houses, but the greater part as granaries or rooms in which the inhabitants deposit their property, when they leave their houses in the town for a warmer situation during the most severe season of the year, when the ravine is nearly choked up with snow, so that *Daba* is only to be considered as a summer residence. The houses are of stone, two stories high, white-washed on the outside below, surrounded with a band of red and *French* grey above, and having terraced roofs surrounded with parapet. The tops of the walls are decorated with lines of pieces of different coloured rags tied to strings. The inside is very filthy ; the floors of little yards, which lead to them, being covered with bones of sheep and goats, fragments of bones, and locks of wool. From the ground-floor, which is raised, a wooden ladder leads to the terrace, which in the *Wazir's* house is divided into an enclosed verandah that serves as a chamber of audience, and into an open space used as a promenade by all the family. The town is divided into three parts, viz. a college, the residence of the *Lama* and his *Gelums*, or monks ; a nunnery ; and the houses of the *Wazir, Deba,* and the laity in general. Immediately in the centre of a semi-circular sweep formed by the houses, are temples or mausolea of *Lamas,* with smaller ones attached to them. These are circular at their base, diminish by smaller circles, and terminate in a point covered by plates of copper, like umbrellas, and gilt : in the centre above these, surrounded by horns, and painted of a red colour, stands an irregular building with one door, and surmounted by a square smaller building, tiled with brass gilt, and decorated with grotesque figures ; it is the temple of *Narayan* or the great spirit. The parapet of this building was adorned with masses of black hair, formed, I believe, of the tails of the *Chouri* cow reversed, plaited and intermixed with pieces of some shining substance, and having on their tops iron tridents.

This morning was dedicated to a visit to the temple, and afterwards to the *Lama.* A priest, by order of the *Lama,* opened a locked door, on which was a ring attached to the centre of an iron embossed shield-like plate inlaid with different metals. This led to the porch of the temple, lighted by an opening in the roof to the East. The side walls were painted *al fresco* on a white ground, with a bold sketch of some deity, with large staring eyes, and enveloped in a kind of glory. The doors being thrown open, we entered an apartment of about 30 feet square, lighted only from the door, and from two large silver lamps on attached pedestals of the same metal, about 18 inches high, placed upon a low japanned stool in the middle of the floor. At the upper end of the temple, and immediately fronting the door, was a figure of *Narayan,* of copper gilt, in the *European* sitting position, and about 20 feet high. The hands were lifted up, with the palms gently inclined forwards, as if in the act of benediction. These, with the feet, were the only parts exposed ; the rest of the figure was draped with narrow robes of silk. On his right hand was a smaller figure of Lacshmi ; and on his left, that of a *Lama* crowned with a conical cap and dressed in pontifical robes. These figures, also well executed, were likewise of gilt copper ; a flight of small benches descended from the feet of each of the last figures, on each side of the room, as low as the foot of the throne, leaving a space clear before. On these was arranged in rows the greatest assemblage of *Hindu* deities I have yet seen. They were of brass, exhibited great variety of countenance, and much better proportion of parts than I have before witnessed. The whole of the group just mentioned were placed in a recess bounded by pillars reaching from the roof to the floor, and separated from the body of the temple by a wooden screen about four feet high, furnished with shelves descending in gradation to the floor. On the upper range were the effigies of deceased *Lamas* carved in wood, with their mothers, and the principal persons of their household ; a large gilt pyramid was on one side of this screen half concealed by a silk veil, and another elevated figure, something like a sceptre on the other ; each on a large gilt stand. Lower down was a gilt chest ; and on the floor, in the space fronting the door, was a low table, on which were ranged several rows of brass, silver, and gilt or golden bowls, containing water for the use of the deity ; a small quantity was poured into my hands, part of which I drank, the rest washed with and threw over my head, as I was directed by the officiating priest : we had a carpet spread on the floor in front of the deity, and immediately under a large expanded umbrella. I had given a present on my first entrance, and afterwards added another trifle for the particular use of the priest in attendance, who desired us to come forward, and examine more minutely the figure of the deity, and receive a portion of his sacred vestments consisting of a stripe of a white silk gauze which was put round our necks. In returning we saw masks of leather in imitation of the heads of stags, tigers, bears, and demons, worn at the celebration of some great festival, ranged on shelves ; and on wooden frames, piles of sheets of writing within small planks of wood, like the boards of books without backs, lying on open latticework tables.

On leaving the temple we were desired to turn some wooden cylinders supported on iron cylinders, in recesses in a wall, and to go round the building seven times, a ceremony which it seems is prescribed to those who wish to have an audience with the *Lama* after a visit to the temple. Whether this was mentioned merely to enhance the sanctity of the place or the personage, or was really the custom, I know not, but the ceremony was interrupted after one round, and setting the whirligigs, by a message from a priest, that Amer Singh was wanted elsewhere. He understood the signal, and went to a small door, which when knocked at, was opened by a laughing ugly fellow, who pointed to four coils of shawl wool, for which a bargain was immediately struck.

We were desired to make another turn round the temple, and were afterwards led up two very steep flights of stairs towards the *Lama's* apartments. Over the first door hung a string to which were attached some leaden pipes, in imitation of the iron ones used for smoking. In an open apartment, up a third flight of stairs, surrounded by a veranda, on a small and thin cushion placed upon an old mat, the bishop of the diocese was seated. We each made a present of a rupee, and three for the *Gelums* ; the latter he would not touch, but sent for the steward to take charge of, and ordered that they should say prayers for us three times ; after which the money should be divided amongst them. His manners were mild and conciliating. To our interpreter he signified that he did not approve of our design of building a hospice at *Mansarovar*. We stated that we should attend to his opinions, even if our money had been in greater plenty than it now was.

At the suggestion of Mr. H., I laid the string of beads, which I usually wore round my neck, at his feet. He was struck with the circumstance, rose, beckoned to two *Gelums* to accompany him, and after a short absence, returned with a pot of sour milk, some butter in a bladder, a kind of cheese and a cake of sweetmeats, which it was signified was considered so good as to be thought worthy of being presented to the deity. He also brought a string of wooden beads, which he desired me to accept, as a mark of friendship, in return for mine, and which I accordingly put on ; we departed highly pleased with the manners of the prelate. In the evening we paid a friendly visit to *Wazir's* son.

July 6th.—Thermometer at sun-rise 46° ; I had caused the pundit and Amer Singh to inquire for wool, in order to purchase a quantity and forward it to *Niti*, and have this day the mortification to find that the people dare not sell any until we shall have received permission to buy from *Ghertope*. This is caused by strict injunctions to all the owners of flocks not to sell any shawl wool except to the *Cashmirians*, or their agents, in consequence of a representation having been made to the Government, that the *Jouaree* merchants had bought some last year, and that the *Cashmirians* would suffer, if any of this kind of wool were to pass into other hands.

During the peroid that the *Undes* was governed by *Rajas* of the *Rajeput* cast of *Surajbans*, and subsequently that it passed under the dominion of the *Chinese*, the independent *Tatars* of *Ladak* were extremely troublesome to the inhabitants by their frequent inroads, and only ceased their depredations in consequence of this country being given in *Jagir* to the *Dela Lama*. The sacredness of this personage, who is the head of the religion of the *Tatars*, caused them to desist from their incursions, and probably, would have the same influence in the event of any alteration in the current of trade: but to this, it is likely, that they would make great resistance.

July 7th.—Thermometer 42°; The *Wazir* made us a visit and staid nearly an hour. I observe, that the priesthood and the immediate officers of Government are in easy circumstances, as also are the gatherds, but the rest of the population are plunged in the most abject poverty, and literally clothed in rages.

July 8th.—Thermometer 46°; at noon in a tent 73°. We have heard that an answer is arrived from *Ghertope*. In the evening I went to inquire the determination of the Government upon our affairs, and was informed that in the following morning the letter should be read to us.

July 9th.—Rained.—Thermometer at sun-rise 50°. It being past eleven, and not hearing any intimation of our presence being desired, I proceeded to the government house, and found the Council sitting, assisted by a number of people whom I had not seen before. I addressed myself to the Council; and as we had been informed that a letter had arrived from *Ghertope*, I begged to learn the sentiments of the Governor in respect to us and their final determination upon them. The *Wazir* said, in reply, that the Governor of *Ghertope* had signified to him that intelligence had been conveyed to him about three years ago, that some *Europeans* were about to come into the country and whether we were the persons alluded to or not, he wished to see us and the goods we had brought, of which he wished he requested an exact inventory to be forwarded to him, and prohibited the sale till he should have inspected them. I told them that although we had suffered much from delays, yet that out of respect for the authority of Government, we were ready to go to *Ghertope* or even to *Lassa*, should it be required of us, as we had no other than honest intentions, but as we were orderd to go by the Government, it was but reasonable that we should be furnished with carriage. After much altercation, it was agreed that cattle were to be ready in three days and that as many as could be procured should be purchased, we taking the responsibility of the measure upon ourselves. In an hour, the interpreter came to say that we should have the requisite bullocks and we are to start in three days from this date.

In the evening we went to see the temple of Narayan again, and to pay our parting visit to the *Lama*. We found the old man in a small cell just large enough to allow of three people sitting down; with a raised bench of brick, fronted by a railing of wood, with a little door in the centre. Although early, he was retiring to rest or meditation and considering the wealth of the college, which is reported to be very great, was a real and edifying picture of humility. He wished to know very particularly if we should return by *Daba*. We answered certainly. He was much pleased with our attention, and putting out his hand to take hold of my friend's white gown, he being a little nearer than me said, " I pray you let me live in your recollection as white as this cloth." There was something particularly affecting in his manner and utterance and I could not help bending out-stretched hand with emotion as I took leave of him.

I mentioned that there are a college and a nunnery. The *Gelums* or monks seem a happy, good-humoured set of people dirty, greasy, and in good case. They carry on a considerable trade in sheeps wool and salt, in exchange for wheat and barley. Of the nature of the institution, I could learn little. Of the *Paraphernalia* of the temple, the resemblance with those of the *Romish* church was very striking. The *Gelums* observe celibacy. There is a nunnery, the rules of which are said to be severe. Commerce with man is punished by solitary imprisonment and a heavy fine.

July 10th.—The mometer 48°. This evening we purposed to mount a hill, on which formerly was a house belonging to the *Raja* and there still remains a temple. In our way, passing close to the house of the *Wazir*, we found him, the *Deba*, and several servants, shooting at a mark with bows and arrows. There was novelty in the contrivance of the target. The bull's eye was composed of two parts, the inner one, about four inches in diameter, was of wood, convex and painted black in the middle with a circle of red on the outside. This was placed in a roll or cushion of cloth which it fitted tightly. The arrows were tipped with wooden balls, some of which were solid and others hollow, with four holes in the end, which caused a whistling sound as the arrow flew through the air. When the arrow missed the target and struck against the butt, it fell to the ground ; if it hit the soft shell of the target, it did not disengage the bull's eye, and no arrow was accounted a shot, but that which dislodged the eye from the target. When struck out, the eye did not fall but dropped a few inches lower than the circle, where it was held by a string from an upper projecting rod. This is altogether not a bad contrivance, as it prevents disputes. These people pull the bow more in the *English* manner than in that of the *Chinese*, their neighbours and masters, but their instruments are very indifferent and they are not formidable archers. They use also the sling, but I had not an opportunity of seeing them exercise with it. Leaving the archers, we ascended to the top of a hill about 300 feet above the level of the lower town, along a zigzag road, and through some winding passages excavated with little art in the strata of gravel and indurated clay. The inside of this temple was by no means so rich as that on the other side, and the priest complained of poverty. He said he felt an interest in our welfare and recommended our departing without delay, as the governing people were not good and we might, if we stayed long, be caught by severe weather and perish. We thanked the old man for his good advice and left him more substantial proof of our regard, for which he was very grateful, and placed round our necks small stripes of gauze. During our stay, the *Gelums* began an evening Hymn which was not unmusical ; but, in a very small cell sacred to Bhavani, three persons were making a noise not unlike the quick chirping of grasshoppers. There were small statues of the last *Surejbans Raja*, his son, daughter, priest, treasurer, and other persons of his court. As it is the custom here for a considerable portion of the property of every person who dies in affluent circumstances, to go to the church, and as likenesses are sent to the priests who pray for the repose of their souls, as in the *Roman Catholic* faith, I apprehend the series of figures represented the whole of the court ; and in this idea my belief was strengthened by observing some females of different age and character on a bench, immediately behind that on which the *Raja* was seated. The head-dress of two of these was very similar to that of abbesses. The *Raja* whose resemblance was here preserved, in consequence of the frequent inroads of the *Ladakis*, and of his father being killed by the *Tatars*, was sent by the principal people to request the protec tion of the *Chinese* who accorded it and assisted him against the invaders. But in an earthquake his house was precipitated, along with himself and his household into the plain, and the *Chinese* afterwards availed themselves of his death to take this country for their own use, and after a certain period to give it to the *Dela Lama.*

At this last temple there were few musical instruments, but at the great one, we saw some prodigiously large brass and copper trumpets made of tubes, which shut in and drew out like telescopes and had small mouth-pieces of pipes, which were distinct. There were also drums of great size set in frames and beat upon their sides.

There are granaries in the rock on which the small temple is situated, in which they say that there are many thousand maunds of rice for the use of the people generally, in the event of any great exigency, and this is certainly a very prudent precaution, as scarcely any grain is raised in this country and the inhabitants are dependent for their annual supply of and barley on the *Marchas* of *Niti* and *Jouar*, Shortly after the period that the *Gorkhas* made an irruption into the territories of the great *Lama*, the *Chinese* government ordered 30,000 maunds of rice to be taken out of the magazine, which is, in fact, property of the public, but how the funds are provided, I did not learn.

July 12th.—Thermometer 51°. The *Chouar* bullocks arrived at day-break ; and having paid for their hire as well as for the food of two horsemen who were to accompany us, into the hands of the interpreter, we struck our tents and took leave of *Daba.* At 4906 paces arrive at the summit of hills, said to contain gold. To the right are clay hills, broken down by melting snow into strange-looking projections and hollows. Scarcely the slightest appearance of vegetation, and yet a hare was seen upon these heights. At 5116 paces reach a narrow pass, through which we go and descend to a stony plain, then enter a very deep water-course, now dry, of which the banks are perpendicular, of vast height, and formed of beds of gravel. I examined their structure with great attention, in hopes of finding some traces of marine productions but was disappointed. At 7230 paces came to a plain sloping to the *Satudra* or *Setlej.* It came from the S.W. by W. and ran N.E., receiving here the *Tiltil* ; breadth 80 yards, depth 3½ feet. The current was so rapid that I could scarcely keep my footing. On the plain were two very beautiful poplar trees, in which were many goldfinches which regaled me with a song, whilst I sat under the shade of the trees, waiting for the party, having reached the river half an hour before they arrived.

The broken ground in the neighbourhood of *Daba* and which we did not lose sight of, until we quitted the bed of the *Tiltil,* was very extraordinary in appearance. The right bank was of great height and the melting snow had cut the clay of which it was formed, into channels, leaving intermediate ridges, which, from difference of hardness or being acted upon by the water in different directions, was fashioned into great diversity of figure, in some places representing castles, fortifications, houses and masses which baffled description.

We have passed three villages today, all painted, and of different colours. These are winter residences of the inhabitants of *Daba* and *Dong*.

Just at the point when we began ascending, the valley narrows suddenly to a channel only just sufficient to give passage to the water. The hills which are stated to be rich in gold, are granite of mixed colours, the red predominating, with horizontal strata of quartz and small fibrous veins of a white material like agate, descending perpendicularly, where the rock has been exposed to the weather, its surface is broken into small pieces, having little more cohesion than clay burnt in the sun. This decomposition is effected, I suppose, in consequence of the different materials of which the mass is composed, not being intimately united and water entering the fissures where it congeals, & c., bursts the structure.

The gold here is separated by washing, there being no fuel, in the neighbourhood or rather no wood ; for, from the appearance of some of the hills, I apprehend that they hold coal. In the bed of the *Setlej*, were many large flowering shrubs, which I take to be a species of the tamarisk. I have found it from three inches high to eight feet, in situations more or less favourable. The yaks and goats were very fond of the foliage. I observed that the bite of the yak is quicker and nearer the ground than any other species of neat cattle I am acquainted with ; a peculiarity which fits them for the short and scanty herbage of an *Alpine* country.

We have descended much to the *Setlej*, notwithstanding the mountains are high, which intervene between this river and *Daba*, and the heat is great. In the tents the thermometer stood at 96°. Distance come this day 7525 paces.

July 13th.—Thermometer at sunrise 56° ; march at 6.30. This plain is stony, about half mile in breadth and length, bounded partly by heights and partly by the *Setlej*. It is full of shallow pits made by persons who have dug for gold-dust, and left heaps of stones by the sides of the excavations. At 306 paces ascend to another flat which has likewise been dug. At 1835 paces reach a small flat, where there has been cultivation ; caves of gold mines in the rock to the left, now deserted. At 5975 paces reach a house, near which are two gold mines with tunnels under the surface. Heretofore the excavations were perpendicular. The earth is dug out and carried to the brook to be washed.—At 6182 paces arrive at the ground for encampment near the village of *Damoo*, situated half-way up a rock on the right bank of a water course, in the direction of which we travelled most part of this day, consisting of a few red houses and many caves, with two or three temples.

In the evening killed seven hares. There are great numbers of these animals. They are short in their bodies, longer in the hind legs and somewhat smaller than those in *England*. Their fur is much finer and longer ; altogether they are much paler generally. The under part of the neck is fawn colour, sides greyish, belly white and the things are furnished with thicker and longer furs than the rest of the body, and of an ash or lead colour mixed with grey. When disturbed, they fly to the mountains but frequently stop and rise on their hind legs to look at their pursuers. Their flesh is well tasted ; and they are very prolific ; as in two there were eight young ones. Some cultivated land under the grain called *adhi jou* well irrigated.

July 14th.—Thermometer 52° ; leave our ground at 5.25. At 5780 paces much saline efflorescence on the ground, supposed to be soda cracked under the foot like slightly frozen earth. The skeletons of two wild horses were lying in the valley. In various parts of the road we have found many skulls of the male *Baral*, with enormous horns. Some have at least been from 50 to 60 lbs. weight. We meet again with rhubarb which we had long lost sight of. At noon, thermometer in the tent 75° : on a high hill to the right, three wild horses suddenly made their appearance, probably for the purpose of coming to water after looking at us for some time, they went off at a smart trot. They were too far off to afford a very clear view, but seemed to be about thirteen hands high, a bay colour ran along the upper part of the neck and back and sides were of a fawn or azure colour. Their heads appeared thick and short, but well carried : their bodies round, short : general shape compact, clean, and tail thinly furnished with hair.

July 15th.—At sun-rise, thermometer 41° ; march at 5.40. At 574 paces a bed of snow in the water-course. The plashes of water on the surface of the ground, melted during the day, are frozen during the night. Road ascends to 1934 paces, when we reach the level of a beautiful plain about a mile and a half broad, with mountains to right and left, and narrowing to a gorge about three miles in front. Mountains on the left have snow falling upon them. At 4800 paces reach the right side of the valley which declines to the North : a stream arises from a bed of melting snow, direction N. 65 E. At 5240 paces a second bed of snow. Middle of valley stony with two currents of water. Animals of a fawn colour, about twice the size of a rat, without a tail and having much longer ears than rats ; *Q. Marmot** ? They burrow in the ground and seem to associate with a smaller species of the same form and general character, but of a much darker colour, perhaps younger ones only. One of this sort was shot yesterday, being taken for a young hare, which it resembles in its mode of jumping and sitting on its hind legs. At 5551 paces the valley narrows to 600 yards, surrounding hills said to contain gold which is sometimes found in lumps of considerable size. At 9786 paces encamp ; at 11 A.M., cloudy, high wind ; begins to rain, afterwards hails and this alternately with strong wind till sun-set, when the atmosphere clears and the wind falls.

July 16th.—Thermometer at sun-rise 34° ; our tents frozen. March at 6.45 along the left bank of the stream which we followed yesterday ; saw close to our ground a large pair of horns attached to a skull which I supposed to have belonged to the *Baral* or wild sheep, but was said by the *Uniyas* to be an animal called *Douga.* At 1905 paces large fragments of frozen snow fallen into the water from the rocks, almost choaking up the channel, which is not above seven yards broad. The frozen snow or rather ice, when broken from the edge of the projecting banks under which the water flows divides into pyramidal or conical nails, the small part downwards. Red

* Probably a new kind ; as all the known species of Arctomys have short ears or none. In other respects seems to agree with the genus.

stones, something libe cinnabar of antimony, with black shining crystals, interspersed through their substance. Large lumps of green granite glazed over, in parts with a kind of green glass, in the bed of the stream. At 2000 paces enter into a narrow defile of frozen snow, which the stream has cut through and deserted. A ledge of about eight feet thick, is suspended to the rock at each side, leaving a narrow passage between them, 94 paces long ; at 2435 paces came to another defile of ice. At 3420 paces, rhubarb plants in plenty. At 6375 paces our stream joins another and the road leads to a plain, on which were two wild horses and a prodigious number of hares. At 8025 paces reach the bed of a clear, broad, and rapid, but not deep river ; plain dug in many parts for gold. Having crossed the river, and reached our ground at 1 P.M. and 11,962 paces, we encamped. We killed this day one hare and two grouse or birds of this class, of a fawn colour, feathered legs, broad feet, covered with a pad of horn, divided into many points, like shagreen, and having two long thin tail feathers. This river which rises near *Gongre*, goes past *Ghertope*, then close to *Latak* or *Ladak*, and is said likewise to proceed to *Bakhara*, where probably it falls into the *Ammoo*. *Djihan*, or *Oxus*. The mountains on each side of this valley or plain, which is about five miles across, dip much to the N.W.

July 17th.—Thermometer 39°. Ice or water near our encampment. Saw some *Brahmini* geese* and small shrikes hovering over the river. At 336 paces ascend the foot of the mount, ranging with the river which runs about eighty yards to the left. At 1360 paces, the plain is divided into an upper step about two miles broad, and a lower one, in which is the river following the middle of the lower step or valley, and about a mile in breadth. Many wild horses on the upper step. At 3200 paces myriads of small flies, very troublesome. At 4205, road very uneven from hillocks and hollows. The surface of the ground covered with salt. At 5720, the various currents which divided the valley unite and form a large and clear

---

* Anas Casarça

stream, of considerable rapidity. At 6000, a very large but dry water-course leads to the river. At 8600, a valley opens from two to three miles broad and covered with large pebbles. Heat very great. At 11278, come to five currents of a river which we cross. This river rises from mountains covered with snow lying S. 75 E., and falls into that just mentioned. *Ghertope*, formed by some black tents, at a considerable distance bears from hence N. 5 E. The intervening plain, and indeed as far as the eye can reach until it is bounded by a pass to the N.W., is covered by prodigious bodies of sheep, goats and yaks, amongst which is a small number of horses. The number of cattle cannot I think be less than 40,000. At 14,000 paces reach the town or rather assemblage of tents in clusters made of blankets surrounded by hair ropes fixed to stakes. Over the tents are variously coloured shreds of silk and cloth as flags.

We had only just pitched our tents, arranged our baggage, when a messenger arrived from the *Deba* and *Wazir*, desiring us to pay them a visit today, and we should proceeded to business the following day ; the terms of the message were too pressing to admit of delay, accordingly we proceeded to the house of the *Deba* with our presents. It was enclosed by a fence about four feet high and surrounded by the same litter of bones, horns and scraps of wool, that we had remarked at *Daba*. After entering an enclosure, we stopped a few seconds at the close of small yard, in the front of which were some matchlocks and bows and arrows, piled in a kind of guard-house and we were desired to go through a lòw door into a room, about twenty feet long. At the opposite end, on a raised bench of earth, covered with a carpet and cushions, sat an elderly man, bare-headed and clothed in a greasy yellow damask gown. This was the *Deba*. On the right hand from the *Deba* was a dark complexioned person who was his younger brother ; and on his right again, a rather fair young man who was the son of the late *Wazir*, and now shared the authority of government with the *Deba*. The *Deba* had rather a shrewd countenance. His brother had a sullen expression and was ill-favoured. The young *Wazir* had a pleasing face, of the *Tatar* kind. We had cushions placed on the side of the room, opposite to the young men and our attendants with those of the household occupied the lower parts of the chamber. Some conversation passed through the medium of our interpreter which turned upon our usual place of dwelling, and the articles we had brought with us, of which an inventory was handed to the *Deba*, and after being looked over by him, given to the *Wazir*. The apartment was built of sods. The roof was flat, made of branches of trees laid across, covered with sods and having a square hole near the centre, which answered the double purpose of letting in light and giving vent to smoke, the sides of the room were hung with dirty yellow silk. On the right hand of the *Wazir* were two dogs. The *Deba* sat at the upper end of the room on a platform of sods two feet high, covered with an old carpet, on a cushion faced with *China* satin. Before him was a little long table, on which a box with barley-meal, a blue and white large *China* tea-cup, a thing like a small lead tea-canister, used as a spitting pot and a greenish jusper tea-cup less than the other. This latter was frequently filled by a boy, from a large earthen tea-pot, with a pale-coloured lid, apparently cold. Superstition in eastern countries attaches to jasper cups the property of splitting, if poison be put into them and this trait, at first blush, does not speak in favour of the morality of our *Tatar* friends.

Over his head, to defend him from the earth of the sods or other annoyance, were two or three pieces of common chintz and at the right corner was a small square apartment, made by a chintz curtain, in which was a light ; as the *Deba* lighted his pipe from a chafingdish of charcoal, which was on the floor, I suspect him to be a worshipper of the long hymns which our attendants chanted on the road, at the first appearance of that luminary.

Our interview was very long but it was easy to see that the impression of our being either *Ghorkhas* or *Felings*, (so the *Tatars* call *Europeans*) wore off either by the representations of the *Deba* of *Daba* or by the weight of our presents. Particular inquiry was made for pearls and cups of crystal. Round the *Deba's* neck was a string of beads, thick in the middle and squeezed in at the ends : each bead about an inch and a half long, of a black substance resembling elastic gum and marked with a deep circular impression made by a kind of seal. At the bottom was a small oblong-rounded gold box, with a little turquoise stone in the middle of the lid. In each ear he had a long pendant, consisting of a large pearl between rows of small turquoise stones set in gold. All the three persons mentioned had on their tail, which is twisted from three plaits, a gold circular ornament in lieu of a rosette. This is generally larger than a crown piece, half an inch thick, with a raised edge defended by very beautiful filligree work enriched with some decoration of the turquoise. This is really an elegant trifle, and with the exception of a dagger case, and an etui for long iron sticks to clean the throat of their tobacco-pipes, was the only real decoration betokening taste, I have seen in the country.

July 18th.—This morning we displayed our goods as detailed in our inventory. After we returned, a *Cashmirian Vakil* from the *Raja* of *Latak* sent word that he was ready to buy our goods if the *Deba* did not close with our terms. He said that he should be glad to open a commerce with *Hindustan* for goods of that country in exchange for the productions of *Latak*. That place, he said, was about sixty cos or ten days' journey from *Ghertope* and the same distance from *Cashmir*. He mentioned a place called *Baschar*, twenty days' journey from *Latak*, and ten only from *Bokhara*. The road through *Cabul*, from *Delhi* to *Bokhara*, he represented as very circuitous. From *Amritsir* to *Latak* the journey was from twenty to twenty-five days and the best season for it was the hot weather or the rainy season, but it would be preferable to go in the former, and return in the latter period. He purchases shawl wool on advances at thirty *negis* per rupee ; the first quality sells in *Cashmir* at twelve *negis* and the second fifteen *negis* per rupee. The best wool comes from the neighbourhood of *Ouprang Kote* near *Manasarovar*.

July 19th.—The *Latakis* as well as the *Uniyas* are not able to grow grain enough for their own consumption, but are supplied by the inhabitants of the hills. The *Uniyas* procure their grain from the *Jouaris*, the *Marchas*, and other traders, through the passes as far as *Beschar,* the *Latakis* from the *Cashmirians.* The supply of grain is highly important to the *Uniyas* as they live on barley-meal and rice which they eat with their tea. Animal food seems to constitute only a small portion of their diet.

The shepherds are now beginning to shear their sheep and goats. *Jouari* and *Baschar* merchants are purchasing sheep wool which they manufacture into *Pankis* and blankets ; and those from *Latak* are collecting the shawl wool. I purchased a small quantity of the latter, at the rate of twentyfive *negis* per rupee. The *Latakis* require thirty. The *Deba* hinted that he might be disposed to give twenty and this in the beginning it may be prudent to take, until a footing be established. It is important to shew that he will receive more advantage by dealing with our agents in future, than with the *Latakis.* These have some shawl goats, but not in number sufficient to supply the *Cashmirian* market. However, if a portion of the quantity raised in *Undes,* can be diverted from the usual line, they may be compelled to keep more goats themselves. Still without much success, as the cold is not so severe in the neighbourhood of *Latak,* as to the eastward, in which direction the mountains are higher and covered constantly with a large quanitity of snow.

July 20th.—At a little distance from us and close to the river, two people are engaged in preparations for making paper. They have two large bags of old paper that has been written upon and manufactured from the bark of the root of the *Latbarua,* formerly mentioned. A few large flat stones are placed near the edge of the water where a portion of the stream has been divided from the main current by a low piece of sods. On the grass are two frames of wood, covered on one side with fine cloth and the other is open, forming a shallow tray. The workmen begin by dipping some of the old paper in the water, then beating it upon a flat stone with a small round one, till it is reduced to a pulp. One of the trays is then placed in the broad part of the canal, leaving a space for the water to run under it. The pulp is put into a geer pump with water, and worked into a paste ; it is then poured on the cloth, and as this is sunk two or three inches in the stream, the water rises through the cloth into the tray and mixing with the pulp, dilutes it. The impurities which swim, are picked out, and the pulp agitated by the hand until it is supposed to be sufficiently clear, when the current of water is lessened. The workman sees if the cloth be equally covered with pulp and if any part look thin, he stirs the water with his finger immediately over another that is too thickly covered and raises a cloud of paste which his finger leads to the thin spot, and by making a little eddy, the motion of which he gradually diminishes, the pulp is made to subside. By a repetition of the simple process, the sheet becomes of an equal thickness throughout ; when it is carefully raised out of the water and placed horizontally on the ground to dry, till the greater part of the moisture is drained off, when it is gradually raised and when nearly dry, the frame is set upright ; when perfectly hard, one corner of the large sheet is raised from the cloth and the whole detached by the hand. However, this paper is very inferior, as to evenness, to that made in *Hindustan.*

July 21th.—At about ten o'clock we were visited by three *Tatar* musicians from *Latak* ; one played on the hautboy, another on drums and the third sung and danced. The airs were very similar to those of the *Scotch* and the tones of the hautboy resembled strikingly those of the bagpipe. This instrument had eight holes for the fingers and one for the thumb, with two reeds and a metal tube, with a broad flange concave upwards and convex downwards, in which the reed was inserted. The reeds were tied together with a piece of string about two inches long, that the loose one might be ready to be changed instantly. The musicians began with an overture not unlike that of Oscar and Malvina, as far as comparison may hold between the execution from two instruments, and that of a full band. They then sang the words without music, and so went on with the instrumental and vocal performance alternately.

The *Deba* and *Wazir* made their present, consisting of two large trays of rice, one coarse, the other fine, three lumps of butter, sewn in skins and eight sheep. The butter was rancid, a circumstance which in this country does not lower its value.

The exhibition of the articles of my small medicine chest and of some surgical instruments, appeared to give much satisfaction and both the *Deba* and *Wazir* were pleased with a few drops of oil of peppermint on sugar.

July 22nd.—This morning I received a message from the *Deba* to visit him as soon as possible. He proposed a new rate of valuation for the coin, in which our advance for wool had been made to him. This proposal was a gross roguery as we had weighed the rupees and found that one of them was equal to 4½ *Lataki Timashas,* and had ascertained the goodness of the silver. He had too, of his own accord, offered to allow that rate. I told him that we had placed the fullest confidence in his honour and had considered the bargain of the day before as binding on both parties ; however, we were in his power and we wished him to receive the twentyfiveru pees which would have arisen out of the transaction as it at first stood in the light of a *nazar*. I declined giving five *Sirinagar Timashas* in lieu of a rupee, as I had been informed that the *Deba* alone refused them and, probably, through the influence of the *Lataki* merchants. During the arguments on this subject, the young *Wazir* spoke to the *Deba* several times in an under voice held down his head, seemed confused, abashed and ashamed of the trick played by the *Deba*. The latter, obviously pleased with having carried his point, said that heretofore no shawl wool had ever been sold except to *Lataki* merchants ; that there was an order of government inflicting the loss of his head on any man that should sell this wool to any other person but that in consequence of our having come from a great distance, being, as he was fully aware, persons of consideration, and as he was pleased with our conduct, he had departed from the general rule and had put us on the same footing with the *Latakis* that we should, in future, be placed on the same terms as they, and he would engage that no third person should enter into competition with the two parties for this article. I expressed my satisfaction with his promises, and begged that he would give me a list of the things he might be likely to want from *Hindustan*, as the *Europeans* sent many articles of great utility and beauty to that country. He said that a sword and large pearls of a rose colour, pear shape and free from flaws or irregularities, would be most acceptable. He gave me a drawing of one, which probably would be worth 2000 rupees, and which he valued at 3 or 400. After our commerical affairs were thus settled, he said that we could not have permission to go out of the usual road from *Ghertope* to *Manasarovar* or to stay more than one or two days at that place. Thence we were to proceed to *Gangri*, afterwards to *Hienlung*, to take up our wool, then to return to *Daba* and enter the territories of the *Gorkhas* by the *Niti* pass. I answered that we were ready to obey, to the utmost of our ability, the orders which he had prescribed but that it had entered into our pilgrimage to visit *Jwalamuchi*, and that by the road of *Niti*, we should make a round, to which our finances were unequal. He said that the heads of the *Seyanas*, who had become sureties for us, should answer for our leaving the country by any other road. I urged every argument that occurred to me, but he was inflexible. He said his own head would be forfeited if he gave his consent to our returning by any other pass and that our lives were held by him in equal estimation with his own, but that the case was without remedy. This blow was unexpected and heavy as it places us in the alternative, either of being exposed to be stopped by the *Gorkhalis* or of losing the benefits of the connexion we have formed with the governor of the *Undes*. Amer Singh says that as the *Marchas* were out security here, so will they guarantee our passing by the *Baschar* road. To effect this he says, it is only necessary to go one day along the *Niti* road when we leave *Daba* and then striking to the West with a good guide, we shall reach the *Baschar* without inquiry or molestation ; or if we dislike that plan, we may go to *Niti*, and make an arrangement with the *Mana Marchas*, near *Bhadrinath*, to give us a guide. My companion thinks it will be best to go as far as *Tapoban*, and there striking over the great snowy *Tunsasi* range, gain the province of *Budan* and push vigorously for *Chilkea*. I prefer this because we can see our cattle safe to *Niti*, and make an arrangement then for passing our cattle and goods through the *Gorkha* territory. The old Pundit opines for the *Baschar* road and says we shall neither be seen nor heard of by the route which he shall chalk out, until we reach a country in which we shall not be noticed, I rather apprehend that the prohibition has been caused by the inquires which the old man has been frequently making from *Baschar* people respecting the state of the road but, be it as it may, it is clear to me that if we wish not to furnish to the governor of *Ghertope* a substantial reason for rejecting future communication with us, we must abide by his order in respect to quitting his country by the *Niti* pass.

Mr. H. went to the *Cashmirian* and found that he was a *Wakil* or agent of the *Raja* of *Latak* for the purchase and sale of wool. He said that the amount of wool annually bought by the *Raja* was between two and three lakhs, the greater part of which was resold to the *Cashmirians* merchants who waited for the return of the *Wakil* and paid for it immediately. Merchants from *Amritsir* took off the rest. In speaking of articles of merchandise which were marketable at *Latak*, he mentioned coral beads, which formerly were brought from *Delhi* and *Benares*, and, though exceedingly dear, were resold into *Tatary* at a great profit. But within the last three years their value has fallen greatly, from the great numbers which have come through *Yarkund*. These have been brought by the (*Ooroos*) *Russians*, who have long been in the habit of trading with that country, and in the course of the last three years have pushed on a lively traffic into *Cashmir* through agents. The *Wakil* said that the *Ooroos* had not yet been at *Latak* ; but the *Deba* of *Daba* asserted, that kafilahs of 5 or 600 *Ooroos* on horseback had come to the fair of *Ghertope*. Now if this latter intelligence be true, the *Russians* must reach *Ghertope* by another route than that of *Yarkund*. The *Wakil* said that the horses of *Latak* were much larger than those of *Undes*, but that the best were bred in *Yarkund*, thirty days' journey from *Latak*, and that *Bokhara* was fifteen days' journey from *Yarkund* : *Latak* is ten or twelve days' journey from *Ghertope*, and the same distance from *Cashmir* and twentyfive from *Amiritsir*. Thus the road to the N.W. of the *Himalaya* from *Delhi*, would stand thus from *Amiritsir* to *Latak* twentyfive days, *Yarkund* thirty, *Bokhara* fifteen, making a total of seventy days, a much shorter distance than that by *Cabul*.—In this route there are two days journey, in which no water is to be met with; and for thirty days there is a track without inhabitants ; but the road is safe. I must here remark that the river, which goes from *Ghertope* to *Latak*, does not proceed to *Bokhara* as before stated; but falls into the *Attock*, or more properly speaking, is the main stream of that river. Neither is it a fact, that *Cashmir* furnishes *Latak* with grain, as was at first reported to me, the latter country having sufficient land in cultivation for producing barley and other grains, except wheat and rice, which it obtains from *Baschar*. I went this evening to the *Cashmirian's* tent, taking with me two small bottles of essence of peppermint and of volatile caustic alkali. He received me with great respect, spoke in the highest terms of the regard shown to medical characters in the West, and of the pleasure he had in our meeting, which he now regretted had not taken place before. His name was Ahmed Khan, Kazalbash, about fortyeight years of age, and of a respectable appearance. He placed before me some fine sugar-candy and a paper of saffron. Looking-glasses of large sizes were, he said, much, in request in *Cashmir*. He was particularly desirous to have a lancet of the same make with one that I had given to the *Garpan*, but in this I could not indulge him. I drew him on to converse about the *Russians*, but could learn no more than what has been stated, save that a few have before been in *Cashmir*. He brought with him shawls of various kinds for sale; and said that his people, who were not come up, had some of great value in charge. Nobody, he said, could trade at *Latak* without the direct permission of the *Raja*. We first supposed, that the *Cashmirians* came to *Undes* for part of the wool they used; and learning that they did not, were disposed to blame them for want of enterprise. However, it appears that they have not been permitted to trade directly with *Undes* by the *Latakis*. A state of warfare had long existed, with intervening periods of peace, or rather truce, between these two states, in the reign of Mahmud Shah. The *Chinese Tatars* then invaded *Latak* whose inhabitants applied to the *Cashmirians* for assistance. These represented their state to the Emperor who ordered them to send some infantry to their aid. By their help the *Latakis* repulsed the assailants; and a treaty of amity was made between the conflicting parties, of which one article was that the shawl wool raised in *Undes* should be sold to the *Latakis* alone. This has since been little infringed upon, except two years ago, when the *Jouari Marchas* purchased a small quantity on account of Mr. Gillman of *Barelly.* The *Latakis* apprized of the transaction, complained to the government of *Ghertope*, who issued the rigorous edict before mentioned, forbidding the sale of any except to the *Latakis*, on pain of death to the party selling.

July 23rd.—Leave *Ghertope* ; thermometer 38° at sun rise. The night has been frosty. Having taken leave of the *Deba* or *Garpan* in the afternoon, and of the *Wazir* at night, we prepared to start. The *Wazir* treated us with much cordiality. He said that in a very short time he should go to *Lassa* to remain. In his apartment, which was a much better one than that of the *Deba*, were many trunks, and in the right hand angle was a small platform with benches in front, on the top of which was a brass image, before which a lamp was burning, and grain of various kinds was served on salvers of wood. On the lowest step were several plain wine-glasses reversed, which, from their clumsiness, I supposed to be of *Russian* manufacture. He shewed us the picture of the late *Lama*, executed in silk ; but both the form of the person and the countenance, announced more of the female than of the other sex. This character I have remarked to have prevailed in every portrait of the many different *Lamas* which I have seen ; and were it not that no mention has been made of this personage having been emasculated, I really should have imagined this to have happened. However, taken out of the hands of his parents in infancy, educated in the entire subjection of the passion of sex, and kept in a state of little less than entire confinement, with full feeding, it is not surprising, that the features of the face should have little of the virile character, and that the whole contour of the body should contract a feminine softness undistinguished by the bold variety of swell and fall belonging to a muscular frame accustomed to exercise.

At 3985 paces reach two piles of stones, the uppermost of which were engraved with a character, that appears different from that in common use, and appropriated I presume, to religious purposes. The valley here narrows and is bounded by mountains, whose tops are more or less covered with snow, and it takes a winding direction to the left. At 5407 paces arrive at our ground of encampment near some tents, and a considerable herd of yaks with a lock of the finest sheep I have seen in *Tatary*. Pleased with the prospect of having my choice from amongst the best collection of cattle of every kind I had seen, I rambled through the whole, and made choice of several female yaks and calves as also of young goats, which however were not equal in quality to the yaks and sheep.

The horsemen, whom I discovered, too late, to be intoxicated, said that they had no orders to allow me to pick out of the flock ; but would send for instructions on that point.

July 24th.—Thermometer 44°. At an early hour ordered the pundit, sircar, and interpreter to proceed to *Ghertope*, and represent to the *Deba* and *Wazir*, how we had been treated ; as also to mention that the horsemen had said, that as they had received only four days' pay, we must travel day and night. We had scarcely determined upon this measure, when the horsemen sent word, that a message was come from the *Deba*, importing that he would send another draft of each kind ; and, if I did not approve of them, I might take back the articles he had purchased. I directed them to offer a higher price for the power of selection ; but rather to take such cattle as he should offer, than on our part to break the original bargain. In the evening my messengers returned with eight-cows, and the same number of calves, of which four were bulls.

July 25th.—Thermometer 41°. March at 8.10. The river we have left comes from N. 85° E. The mountains in this thoroughfare for the most part covered with snow. The breadth of the valley in which the stream runs, is about 3 1/2 miles. Thermometer at 1 P.M. 82°. The road on which we are proceeding seems a great thoroughfare ; many *Baschar* and *Jouari* merchants having passed today with loaded sheep, goats, and yaks, towards *Ghertope*.

July 26th.—Rain. Thermometer 43°. The changes of temperature in this climate are extremely sudden. Last night the mountains to the right were bare; this morning they were covered with snow. Thermometer in tent 74°, at three P.M. rain; alternate sun-shine, overcast sky, wind, and thunder.

July 27.—Thermometer 39°. At noon, all our baggage being dry, commence our march. The river from this spot runs N. 70° W. about 1 3/4 miles, and then takes a turn to S. 80° W., and joins the river along which we went to *Ghertope.* At 4460 paces cross the river three feet deep, rapid, with large slippery stones; water very clear. At 6260, thirteen wild horses grazing to the left. At 7957, came to the bank of the river, which we cross, about 2 1/2 feet deep, 80 yards broad, and very rapid. At 8200, reach our ground and encamp. The valley well furnished with grass. Several *Tatar* tents, and cattle grazing. Much furze on the adjacent hills River comes from N. 75 E., and runs N. 50 W. for about 1 3/4 mile, when it takes a turn to the S. 75 W. and forms one of the principal branches of the *Ghertope*, supposed to belong to the *Attock.* Wind very cold, raining all around. The river rose rapidly, and the *Tatar* horsemen refused to cross their horses, in order to bring over some of the people who had stayed to conduct our goats and sheep across the river. The yaks were sent in, who stemmed the current. Some clung to the tails of the animals and came over easily; the others, more timid, preferred retreating to some huts at a distance, where the *Tatars* gave them milk and lodging. A few drops of essence of peppermint on sugar to the *Hindus*, and a dram of brandy to the *Musselmans*, with strict injunctions that they should run about and not approach the fire till warm, prevented any of the persons who had been much exposed to the cold from suffering by it.

July 28th.—Thermometer at sun-rise 44°; obliged to wait until ten o'clock, before the river had sunk sufficiently to admit of the men, and a few goats which were left, passing over. At 1. 20 march. The mountains have the particular red appearance indicating the presence of gold; and though adorned with little verdure, are picturesque in their forms. Cross several small rivulets which come from the left, and fall into several ponds to right : air very cold. At 7050 paces reach a pile of stones covered with inscriptions. At 8160, road crosses several dry watercourses, and ascends to the summit where are two small heaps of stones, over which is a line covered with slip of rags, and supported by two sticks. At 9460 paces cross a rivulet formed by fresh-melted snow. This rises on the left and runs to the right. Reach our ground, 10,066 ; at 5.20 very cold, windy and cloudy. A storm rises in the N.W. attended with thunder and small hail. Thermometer 47. Hail changes to rain, which falls steadily till 7 P.M.

Today I heard a strange, sharp and loud noise proceeding from the side of a hill, at the bottom of which the road ran. It seemed between a bark and a howl, and expressed much anger. For some time I could not make out whence it came, but, whilst casting my eyes on a furze bush, an animal about the size of a middle-sized dog sprung from a hole underneath it, about fifty yards up the hill, and after surveying the passengers and repeating his yelping, retreated with precipitation into his cave, as soon as he saw me jump from the back of a *Chownr*. His general colour was a yellow brown. His head was round with small ears, his face burned light and dark-yellow and his tail long.

July 29th.—Thermometer 37°. At 9.45 it began to hail, which soon changed to rain, and lasted until 10. We began our march at 10.45. Mountain on the left covered with snow : many wild horses grazing on the high Table Land. At 16,652 paces, reach a branch of the *Satudra* river which I forded here, and again at 16,868, much against my will, as it was extremely cold; but my yak had played some tricks, which in my weak state of health I did not think prudent to experience more than once. At 7.15 reach *Masar*, very cold and much fatigued. Thermometer 46°.

July 30th.—Halt at *Misar*. Thermometer 44°. In the forenoon, 8 yaks arrived ladden with shawl wool and accompanied by two persons on horseback, one of these was an officer called a *Nerba*, who had received orders from the *Garpan* to supply the quantity for which we had made advances. The morning was hot, a circumstance in our favour, as the sellers of wool are in the habit of wetting it, under an idea, as they pretend, of its twisting the closer, but more probably to make it weigh heavier. However, after a little delay on our part, that the wool might dry as soon as possible, we had it weighed by a pole with a weight, on the principle of the steel-yard, which the *Garpan* had sent with us. As more was brought than we advanced for, we agreed to take it, on the principle of encouraging *Garpan* to give more another year. The surplus amounted to 38 rupees and 1 *Timasha* ; and the *Garpan* had ordered rupees alone to be received, which shewed that he had given directions for more to brought than we had contracted for, in order to try whether we really meant to purchase or used the plea merely in his presence to mask other designs. At this place we found many *Jouari* and *Dhan* merchants, who were troublesomely inquisitive as to who we were, what could be our motives for coming, why we purchased shawl wool. The sight of some of our wares seemed to convince them, that we were what we appeared to be. I consider this day as the epoch at which may be fixed the origin of a traffic which is likely to be extremely beneficial to the Honourable Company.

Misar has only one house, made of bricks baked in the sun, and 5 tents of goat-herds : it is situated upon a rising ground upon the left bank of a rapid stream, forming one of the branches of the *Satudra* or *Setlej.* This stream comes from N. 86.5 E. and runs down a valley about 2½ miles in breadth and near 8 in length, running S.W. After a course of about ½ mile, it joins that which we forded yesterday.

July 31st.—Thermometer 34°. Ice ⅜ of an inch thick. The changes of temperature, so frequent and rapid in this climate, require that the quardrupeds naturally belonging to it should have some very warm clothing, to protect them against their ill effects ; and we find that this has been very liberally bestowed by nature. The sheep has a very thick and heavy fleece ; the goat has at the root of his long shaggy hair a very fine fur interpersed generally ; the cow has a material of the same kind, not much inferior in warmth and softness, which I apprehend might prove a substitute for beaver ; the hare has her fur of peculiar length and thickness ; and even the dog has a coat of fur added to his usual covering of hair. The wild horse (*Equus Quagga*),[3] the wild ass (*Goorkhen, Onagre*), and I believe the mule, the offspring of these animals,[4] are found in abundance on the mountain of *Tatary* ; but whether they have any thing of the fur kind I cannot say but that animal, which is here called the *Baral*,[5] and which seems to have many characters of resemblance to the deer as well as to the sheep, has certainly at the bottom of the brittle hair of the former the most beautiful brown fur I ever saw.

This morning the *Nerba* came to take leave of us, and as his behaviour had been uniformly attentive I was desirous of shewing him that we were sensible of it, and accordingly gave him a double-bladed knife and my sword. The latter was, in fact, no great gift, as it was bought at *Najibabad* for three rupees, and was intended solely for the journey. He was however, highly pleased with the compliment. His name was Thar Chand ; and he said, that he was in the suite of the *Wazir*, and should accompany him to *Lassa*. He wore a pendant in one ear, in which, along with rows of small turquoises, the never-failing ornament of this part, was a large irregular pearl, such as are in high request in this country, on -account of their size. These I understand are brought to *Calcutta*, in considerable numbers during the rainy season, from the *Lackadive* islands, and sold at a very easy rate. The *Nerba's* outer garment was woollen, of green, red, blue, and yellow narrow stripes, manufactured at *Guinak* ; under this were four other garments ; and both men and women constantly load themselves with several vests to prevent suffering from the cold.

On the back of this habit, and on the right shoulder were sewed the saw, adze, chisel, rule and all the insignia of Free Masonry in iron ; the symbols of a fraternity, of which he

---

3. Probably *Equus Caballus*, which inhabits in the natural state, the deserts of great Tatary, 'C.
4. *Equus Hemionus* ; which much resembles the mule. C,
5. *Ovis Ammon*? C,

said he was a member. I purchased from him some gold-dust at the rate of 40 *Sirinagar Timashas* for the *Fitauk* of 7 *Mashas*. The *Nerba* appeared to have gold-dust to the amount of about 5000 rupees ; and it was understood, that every person, willing to become an adventurer in the gold mines, pays to the chief of the district one *Fitauk* as an entrance fee, and all lumps above a certain weight. This occupation is more profitable here, than in most other places ; as though the gold-digger works only three months, he expects that the result of his labour should keep him the whole of the year. Leave *Misar* at ten A.M., having loaded our wool upon the yaks which brought it, and for the hire of which the *Nerba* would receive no gratification ; the first instance of disinterestedness, I have witnessed in this country. At 4500 paces enter *Tirtapuri.* At 4525, pass several piles of stones inscribed as is usual, and some figures carved in stone and painted, Reach the summit of the height at 4575 paces and encamp.

Tirtapuri is the residence of a *Lama* and several *Gelums*, who live in separate houses made of rough stones, and follow a pastoral life. It is perched upon the top of an eminence, about 200 feet higher than the plain, and has Table land running from it eastward. Steep, craggy, lime stone rocks in a state of decomposition immediately overhang it, threatening some of the houses with destruction at no distant period. Insulated pillars, which have resisted the influence of the weather longer than the softer portions of stone by which they were surrounded, seen upon the very point of falling ; but apparently give no alarm to the inhabitants. Still higher, and losing their heads in the clouds, are pointed mountains, which from their brilliant whiteness, appear to consist of chalk, covered here and there with a layer of yellow ochre. Immediately at the foot of the rock, on which the buildings stand, runs a very rapid stream, which is said to proceed from a lake at the foot of the *Himalaya*, called *Rawanhrad* and to constitute the principal branch of the *Satudra*.

To the west of the town, and about a quarter of a mile distant, are the hot springs, forming one of the most extraordinary phaenomena, I have ever witnessed. From two months, about 6 inches in diameter, issue two streams, bubbling about

4 inches higher than the level of the stony substance whence they escape. The water is very clear, and so hot, that the hand cannot bear to be put into it for an instant ; and a large volume of smoke curls round them constantly. They burst forth from a table of calcareous stone nearly half a mile diameter, and raised in most places ten or twelve feet above the plain on which it stands. This has been formed by the deposit from the water of the springs whilst cooling. Immediately surrounding the springs, the stone is as white as the purest stucco. The water flowing over a surface nearly horizontal, as it escapes from the vents, forms shallow basins of different size and shape. The edges of all these basins are curiously marked with indentations and projections, like the tops of mushrooms and fleurs-de-lis, formed by calcareous matter prevented from uniting in one uniform line by the continual but gentle undulation of the water entering into and escaping from the several basins which are emptied by small and successive falls into the surrounding plain. By degrees, however, the fringed edge becomes solid, and contracting the basin of which the hollow fills likewise, the water takes a new course and makes new reservoirs which in their turn become solid. Although the water appears perfectly transparent, the calcareous earth, which it deposits, is of different colours ; in the first instance, near the mouth, it is delicately white without a stain : at a little distance it assumes a pale straw tint ; and further on, a deep saffron hue : in a second the deposit has a rosy hue, which, as it recedes from the source, becomes of a deeper red. These various colours are deposited in the strata, which hardening, retain the tinges they received when soft ; and give rise to variously stratified and veined stone and marble. The whirls, twists, knots, and waves, which some of the fractured edges exhibit, are whimsically curious, and shew all the changes which the stony matter undergoes, from soft tufa to hard marble. I observed that the marble is generally formed in the middle of the depth of the mass, rising up with nearly a perpendicular front of the height before mentioned ; the table must have been the work of ages. The calcareous matter, which is so largely dissolved and suspended by the water whilst hot, is probably furnished by the chalky mountains above

Tirtapuri, but the origin of the heat, I have no clue to discover. The water must be most strangely situated, for two streams so inconsiderable to throw down such a prodigious quantity of earth ; and the surface where quiet is also covered with a thin crust of semi-transparent matter like that which rises on super-saturated lime-water.

At this place, I left the wool which I had obtained at *Misar*. The *Lama* was absent when I took the liberty of depositing the wool in the verandah of the temple of one of the deities therefore it remains to be seen, should he return before I do, how he may approve of this step. However, from what I have seen of the priesthood here, they are an inoffensive class.

Nearly opposite to his house, is a broad wall of stone 150 yards long and 4 feet broad, covered with loose stones inscribed with prayers. The length of time which must have elapsed, before such an extent of surface could have been so decorated by the hands of pilgrims, shows the great antiquity of *Tirtapuri*. There are many little *Maths* having niches in one side, in which are impressions, in unburnt clay, of *Lamas* and deities, and on some of the piles of stones are figures of *Lamas*, of *Narayan*, and of *Bhasmasur*, carved on large flat pebbles.

4

JOURNEY TO LAKE MANSAROVAR : AUGUST 1ST TO AUGUST 31ST

August 1st.—Thermometor 40°. Leave the yak, cows, calves and my goats. Commence our march at 10 A.M., meet a party of *Unias* going with several loaded yaks to the fair at *Ghertope*. The manes of the yaks were died yellow with the *Geru* earth. At 12,800 paces come to our ground and encamp in a green pleasant spot, in a hollow surrounded with many spring, at 4.30 P. M. At 8 P. M., Thermometer 46°.

August 2nd.—Thermometer 32°. A severe frost during the night :—ice a quarter of an inch thick over standing water. March at 10.20. At 10,825 paces a large sheet of remarkable blue water, at the foot of the mountains to the right, called *Rawanhrad*, said to give rise to the principal branch of the *Satudra*, and to communicate by a river with the lake *Mansarowar*, named by the natives *Mapang*. *Rawanhrad* bears S. 25 E. distant 8 miles. At 16,827 paces halt and encamp at 5 P. M, At 7 P. M. thermometer 47°. This day we saw more wild horses than on any former one, also several wild asses of the kind called *Gurkhar*, and likewise I believe some mules. The asses are a little less than the horses. Sam likewise *Barals* and many yaks.

August 3d.—Slight frost, thermometer 34°. March at 9.50. At 7287 paces, cross a stream over a wooden *sankhoo*. At 7325 encamp on a high spot. This is *Gangri* or *Darchan*. There are four houses of unburnt brick or stones, and about twenty-eight tents, amongst which that of the servant of the *Lataki* agent is apparently the best. Sixteen years ago, the old Pundit says, this was a place of consequence. There we find many *Juari* and *Dhermu* merchants with grain, and three tea merchants, who say they are acquinted with *Pekin* which they call the capital of *Mahachin*: but they themselves reside two months journey beyond *Pekin*. *Tatars* of the districts we have seen wore their hair plaited : these people had it cut all round, so that it hung low and loose in their necks, and they wear coats of kid skins made soft-by rubbing, and the hair turned inwards.

A cascade issues from the rocks just above *Darchan*, and falls into the *Rawanhrad*, which is supplied by the melting of the snow on the great mountains at the foot of which it is situated. It is said to surround a considerable extent of mountains, insulting them completely; but this, being the relation of natives, is to be received with caution.

August 4th.—Thermometer at 7 A.M. 57°. We were resolved to stay here today to recruit my strength, which stood much in need of it after frequent attacks of illness.

August 5th.—Thermometer 48°. Leave *Darchan* or *Gangri* at 10.33. At 2675 paces cross a strean which in five or six branches comes from the *Cailas* mountains and disembogues itself into the *Rawanhrad*. At 13.235 paces reach the top : see a fine looking wild horse. Descend to five tents : a wild ass grazing close to us, and a prodigious flock of sheep and goats. The lake of *Mansarowar* or *Mapang* now appears at the foot of a long declivity of pasture bounded by immense mountains towards the South, and, having in front terraces of stone with the usual inscriptions, and a house inhabited by *Gelums*.

August 6th.—Halt on the bank of the lake *Mansarowar*. Morning early, thermometer 47°. This lake is considered as the most sacred of all the places of worship in the opinion of the *Hindus*, founded probably on the difficulty of access to it, not merely on account of its distance from *Hindustan*, and the ruggedness and dangers of the road, but from the necessity of every pilgrim carrying with him money and provision, which latter he must occasionally eat without any preparation on account of scarcity of wood. Few *Jogis* can afford the expense of this journey ; and I met with two on the road, who must have returned for want of funds if I had not borne their expenses. The name is derived from *Man*[1] and *sarowar*, a *Sanskrit* word signifying a lake. The story upon which this appellation is founded is related at great length in the *Sastra*. Why it is called *Mapang* by the *Unias* or *Chinese Tatars*, I have not been able to learn : but it is considered by them an act of religious piety and duty, that the nearest relation of a dead person should carry a portion of the ashes of the deceased, and empty them out of a small bag into the lake, as is practised at *Hardwar*.

Hindu geographers have derived the *Ganges* the *Satrudra* and the *Kali* or *Gogra* from this lake ; and as I believe no *Europeans* ever before visited it, I was anxious to ascertain whether it really gave rise to the two last mentioned rivers or not. As to the former, it is quite clear from the observations made in this journey, coupled with those in the trip undertaken at the suggestion of the late Colonel Colebrooke, by Messrs. Raper, Webb, and Hearsay, that the *Ganges* derives its supplies from the melted snow of the mountains of the *Himalaya*, and a thousand small streams, which fall into its various branches during their passage from these stupendous rocks, to the great common mouth at *Hardwar* : and that it does not receive the smallest streamlet from their extreme Northern face, nor from a source to the Northward of them.

Harballabh, the old pundit, reported, that near the South-western corner, a river issued from it, which flowing in a westerly direction went along the *Rawanhrad*, and escaping from its Western extremity near the foot of the great mountain, formed the first branch of the *Setlej*. Yesterday evening I mounted upon a very high bank, and thought that I perceived distinctly the whole of the line of the shore, without seeing any

---

1. At full length *Manasa*, divine made by Brahme, named Manas, the mind, emphatically. C.

outlet, with the exception of a space near the S.W. angle which a projecting rock concealed from my view. Determined not to leave this point in doubt, I took a fishing rod and gun, thinking that I should have time to amuse myself a little in one or other diversion and return by the evening. At about ten I began my march ; and, although very weak from the frequent attacks of fever to which I had lately been subject, I felt confidence that I should accomplish the object without any material degree of fatigue. As we were encamped about the middle of the northern side, I walked along the shore towards the West. The beach was formed of fragments of stones rounded, and thinned when of small size, by the continual action of the waves : but in some places great masses of red and green granite, marble, and lime-stone, had fallen from the face of the rock, which in many parts was 300 feet perpendicular. These stones, frequently washed by the surf, and glazed by the sun, afforded a very unsafe footing : however, at this time it required only care to prevent falling, which would have endangered a limb, as some of the spaces betwixt the stones were very deep. The steep bank was here and there cut by profound and precipitous watercourses, now dry ; but occasionally serving to convey the snow-water from the high tables upon the head of the bank into the lake. The front of the bank at the height of from ten to thirty yards, had houses of loos e stones and wood built in recesses upon ledges ; but, as there were no stairs to them, I thought them inaccessible to human beings, except by means of ladders, of which I saw none. They were inhabited, as I beheld smoke issue from many, and are I presume the secluded retreats of monastic recluses of both sexes. One of these nuns accosted me by the name of *Guni Lama*, and returning along with me, pointed to one of the rock habitations, which I concluded to belong to her, and appeared by her gestures to invite me to it. However I was so ungallant as to refuse the lady's hospitality : for I cannot suppose that she had any other motive for her civility than to offer me refreshment, or to ask charity, the disposition to which, the view of the inconveniences she was subjected to, by such a lodging, might possibly excite. A weather-beaten face, half stripped of its natural covering by the joint action of a hot sun and cold wind, blistered lips, a long bushy beard, and mustachios, in a country where the former is carefully plucked out, with a gait not of the firmest, had probably raised emotions of pity, and induced her to think I might stand in need of repose. Be it as it may, with the most cordial salutation and expression of thanks by dumb show, I took my leave, and went on with my survey.

After an hour's walk, the beach changed to a deep sand, in some places pure and in others mixed with pebbles. That on the water's edge was bordered by a line of wrack grass, mixed with the quills and feathers of the large grey wild goose, which in large flocks of old ones with young broods, hastened into the lake at my approach ; and though I fired several times with buck shot, few took effect, from too great distance. These birds, from the numbers I saw, and the quantity of their dung, appear to frequent this lake in vast bodies[2], breed in the surrounding rocks, and find an agreeable and safe asylum, when the swell of the rivers of *Hindustan* in the rains, and the inundation of the plains, conceal their usual food. Many aquatic eaglesperched upon the crags of rock ; and several kinds of gulls skimmed along the skirts of the water. An unusually large body of great black gnats along the beach rendered walking troublesome, from their aiming to get into the nose, mouth, and eyes ; but, when the wind lulled, which it did for half an hour, they flew along the surface of the water, and became the prey of a kind of trout without scales, which rose at them with extra ordinary voracity, and with which water seemed to be literally alive. I hoped by rounding the N.W. corner to have had sport by throwing across the wind ; but it then suddenly chopped about, and a heavy surf beat upon the Western shore. As the bank approached this angle, it declined to gentle elevations, leading to interrupted Table Land, and at its base was a large bay, from the bottom of which rose a pyramidical red rock, connected with a line of ridge of high land to the higher flats to the North, and steep towards the South. Upon this was the house of a *Lama* and many *Gelums*, pitched

2. From the known resort of the grey goose (the swan of *Hindu* poets) to this lake, the bird is called in poetic language *Manasaucas*, or he, whose abode is the *Manasa* lake *Am. Cosh.* b. 2. c.v.v. 23. C

in situations which produced a romantic effect, not a little heightened by streamers of various coloured cloth and hair, floating from high poles fixed from the corners and roofs of the houses. Leaving this and diverting my steps to the South, I went along the base of granite rocks amongst such troublesome rugged and slippery stones, as had interrupted my progress in the outset, till I reached a hight, level, and firm bank, which separated the water of the lake from that which accumulated by the slope of the surrounding upland, directing the melted snow into it. At the end of this natural barrier, I saw a point of rock running into the lake, from the top of which I flattered myself, I should have a prospect that would command the whole of the shore to the S.W. corner, and put an end to a task which I now found somewhat too much for the little strength I possessed. But I was severally disappointed : for on mounting a steep hill, of which the point in question formed the front to the lake, another large mountain intervened to prevent my view, with a deep valley between it, and that which I had too hastily concluded would finish my labour. When I had reached the summit of this, another equally high presented itself. My servants were much fatigued ; for my own part, I was obliged frequently to lay down : and it was four o'clock when I reached a small religious pile, whence I got a fair sight of the shore I was so anxious to see, with the exception of a very small portion that was intercepted by the projection of a high bluff angle starting into the lake : unable to proceed from the aching of my limbs and intense thirst, which I could not gratify, I sent a trusty *harkarah* to explore the angle which was concealed from my sight. The sky, which had frequently been overcast and disturbed with violent gusts of wind, now became clear, and sunshine illuminated the whole of the circumference of the lake, so as to enable me distinctly to define every portion of its shore close to the edge of the water, and up to the foot of the mountains by which it is embayed, with the exception of the point to which I had directed the *harkarah* to proceed : there were numerous traces of watercourses leading into it, the most important of which was the *Krishna* sweeping down a ravine between two high mountains of the *Himalaya* range, and expanding like a sheet as it approached the verge of the lake ;

but not a break, nor any other appearance indicated the escape of any river or even of any small stream from it. Although this was clear enough to the naked eye, I employed a telescope and this as well as the evidence of two servants who gave me an account of what they saw, shewed that the *Mansarowar* sends out no rivers to the South, North or West.

At half past four I began to return and descended to the shore which was a bed of round pebbles that had fallen from the side of the mountains. Large masses of these stones, imbedded in a hard cement like old firm mortar, in some places obstructed the path which apparently was more used by yaks than trodden by the feet of man. I was in hopes that I should be able to reach the N.W. corner before the fall of night, and by ascending the high Table Land that formed the summit of the Northern bank, avoid the deep sand and dangerous stony beach which I had traversed in the morning. Walking upon a flat surface, in some degree relieved the active aching and spasms of the thighs and legs, brought on by great exertion in climbing and descending, but did not take away the soreness of the muscles. However, I laboured to the utmost extent of my power, but was much impeded in my progress by a strong wind which poured into the lake with vast impetuosity from the West and rendered breathing difficult. Since morning the wind had shifted four times and had only been a little still for half an hour. In spite of all my endeavours, I could not attain the granite rocks to the S. of the *Lama's* house before night came on, and by another sudden change of the wind, the surf was thrown so high on the shore as to efface all traces of the path, and leave scarcely room enough to pass between the face of the rock and the water. In a small recess we lay down for a few minutes and as I had not seen the surface of the high land on the North, and the night was dark, I thought it on the whole, more advisable to encounter the fatigue of wading through the deep sand and the risk of injuring our legs and feet amongst the stones, than have the chance of falling over the precipice of the rock or into any of the deep ravines by which its surface was broken. But there was another inconvenience that was unforeseen and very annoying. The wind had put in motion the dry sand on the western extremity of the northern shore, and this rose into our eyes and almost blinded us. The servants who were with me, had eaten nothing since the day before ; I had only taken a cup of tea in the morning ; and, though in health, they were little less exhausted than myself. For my part, from the violent pain in my limbs and the singularly accelerated action of breathing, I was compelled to sit down every ten or fifteen minutes ; and was in one of these halts overtaken by my *harkarah* who reported that he had gone nearly to the foot of the *Himalaya* mountains covered with snow and had not seen the smallest trace of any river issuing from the lake. At half past eleven, benumbed with cold, and completely overcome with fatigue, I reached my tent, where a cup of warm tea was a most welcome refreshment.

August 7th.—Thermometer 49°. Found my eyes inflamed and observed that those who were with me, had also suffered in the same organ. Sent for Harballabh, and observed to him that the river which he had crossed on *Sankhos* sixteen years ago, did not, as he supposed proceed from *Mansarowar*, but from some part of the *Himalaya* to the west, and taking suddenly a western course, fell into *Rawanhrad*, and led him into error on this point. He was very positive on the subject ; said he could bring the evidence of all the inhabitants of the neighbourhood in support of the truth of his assertion and that my *harkarah* had not gone as far as I ordered him to do. To settle this matter, the same *harkarah* and Har Deo, the young pundit, were directed to proceed as far as the south-west corner. At half past eleven at night, they returned much fatigued, and suffering from the cold. They stated that they had gone beyond the south-west corner, and within 500 paces of the *Krishna* river on the south side, without finding any appearance of a river issuing from the lake or of any former bed of a river which had escaped from it. The distance of the *Lama's* house from our encampment was 3521 paces; from the former place to the foot of the mountain, from the top of which I made my survey 12,500 paces : they went 5000 paces farther, making in the whole 21,621 paces or about eighteen *English* miles ; which, doubled by their return, made their day's journey thirty six miles. According to their calculation, my journey consisted of twenty four miles, but adding the crossing of the hills or may fairly be estimated at three more. The distance altogether is but trifling ; yet the circumstances of my weakness from previous illness, the badness of the road, being benighted, & c., rendered its performance very dressing. However, the fact of *Mansarowar* giving rise to no large river, has been ascertained by it. The old pundit remained much dissatisfied with the decision, and a *Lataki* traveller asserted that eight years ago the stream, which he mentioned, actually existed ; and that at since that period dried up, and the bed has filled. Perhaps an earthquake may have been the agent in this effect. I believe the period assigned tallies with that whom was so mischievous at *Sirinagar*, and it might have extended to this place.

Mansarowar or *Mapang*, of which we had no means of ascertaining by astronomical observation, the exact geographical situation is bounded on the south by the great *Himalaya*, which pours its liquified snow into its basin ; on the East by a prolongation of the *Cailas* ridge ; and on the north and west by very high land under the form of mountian, table, ravine and slope, all declining towards it. In form it appeared to me oblong ; the sides of the east, west and south, nearly straight ; that of the north and especially to the north east where there is a plain at the foot of elevated land, indented and irregularly tending to the east. The angles were not sharp or its figure would have approached nearer to a square than any other ; but it may be considered as an irregular oval. Its breadth from south to north, I estimate at about eleven miles, its lenght about fifteen. The water, except where disturbed by the wind near the beach where it is sandy, is clear and well tasted. No weeds are observable on its surface, but grass is thrown upon its banks from the bottom. The middle and sides farthest from the spectator reflect green ; and taken altogether, it has a noble appearance, whether in an agitated or a quiet state. We had, however, but little opportunity of seeing it unruffled, for the changes of temperature of the atmosphere are here extremely frequent and sudden, attended with great mutability in the wind. Considering the heat of the sun in the middle of the day, the vast bodies of snow on the summits of the neighbouring mountains, which produce their influence when the sun begins to decline and the breaches and gulleys through the ranges of hills, it is not surprising that there should be an almost continual conflict between opposite currents of air, or that the shifts of temperature should be frequent and great. At what season this large basin is most full, I could not learn ; but I apprehend this must be the driest season, as the greatest part of the water, courses which I saw were dry. But I found no appearance of water-mark above four feet higher than the present water line ; which would be wholly insufficient to produce any overflow of its banks.

I saw a great number of skeletons of yaks between the low and high water-mark ; and, although the bones of the trunk and limbs were bare and bleached, the head was in almost every instance, and particularly its fore parts, covered with the skin, to which the hair adhered. I could get no account of the cause of the number of the carcases ; but think it probable, that in the severe season the space between the banks and the water is filled by drifts of snow, and that the yaks going towards the lake fall into them, and are suffocated. Adverting to the instinct and experience of this animal, this solution may be erroneous ; but I have none better to offer. At first it occurred to me that they might have been sacrificed : however inquiry did not bear out this conjecture ; nor could I discover any ground for thinking that these creatures are subject to epidemical diseases, which might have compelled them to resort to the lake, either to quench their thirst, or to alleviate their sufferings by bathing. With regard to the preservation of the skin in the forepart of the head, this would soon dry from the influence of alternate heat and cold, there being little muscular substance between it and the bone to become soft and enter into putrefaction.

August 8th.—Begin to return towards *Hindustan*. Thermometer 45°. Mr. H. cut his and my name on a stone, and left it in a secure place. At eleven A.M. march. At 9100 paces pass tents of *Tatars* and *Juaris* : cross a watercourse, at 10,200 paces, which was dry, when we went towards *Mansarowar*, but is now two feet deep. At 12,126 paces encamp near seven or eight tents. The valley of *Gangri* is about twelve miles broad, and nearly twenty four long. At the eastern extremity is *Mansarowar*: opposite is *Rawanhrad*. The latter lake has always been represented as surrounding some large portions of rock, a little detached from the great *Himachal*; however, the view which I had of it, completely destroys this idea. It consists of two legs which are long and not very broad; one leg runs eastward towards *Mansarowar*, is straight and ends in a point, the other goes to the south amongst the hills; and their divergence forms an angle almost directly opposite to the town of *Gangri* or *Darchan*. I think I saw a stream issue out of it at the western side of this angle, which probably communicates with the many streams which form the *Setlej*; but this point I purposed to make out decidedly.

August 9th.—Thermometer 42°. I suffered much from fever and was unable to go to *Rawanhard*. About sun-set wind became very high and thick clouds with loud peals of thunder, announced the approach of a storm. This began with hail, turned to rain, and at midnight a fall of snow took place, which lasted till morning.

August 10th.—At six in the morning, thermometer 32°. Our tents covered two inches thick with snow which continues to fall. The streams on the plain much swollen, many parts covered with water that were quite dry yesterday. The ground very poachy, all prospect of visiting *Rawanhard* given up and anxiety felt, lest a continuance of this weather should fill the passes of the *Himachal* with snow and exclude us from *Hindustan*. *Rawanhard* receives many rivulets from the southern face of the *Cailas* ridge; but a large body of water, it is probable, fall into it from the northern front of its snow-capped neighbour the *Himachal* range. I much regret to leave unsettled the question of a branch of the *Satudri* proceeding from it, but must bow to the necessity of the case.

On its banks vast numbers of wild geese are bred and it is probably better stored with fish than *Mansarowar*, as one edge of its banks is fringed with grass of considerable height and there is swampy land at the mouths of the streams, which empty themselves into its bosom. At a distance its water was of an indigo blue. The eastern leg appeared about five miles in length ; of that of the southern one I could form no opinion as it was lost in the mountains. The name is derived from *Rawan*, so much famed in the *Ramayana*, and the *Sanscrit* word *hrad*, signifying lake. The principal streams which rise in the *Cails*, and disembogue, are 1st, the *Siva Ganga* ; 2d, *Gauri Ganga* ; 3d, *Darchan Gadrah* ; 4th, *Catyayani*, and there are many others without names. It is said to be four times as large as *Mansarowar* ; but of this I can give no opinion. We have been forced to remain here all day. At nine the snow ceased to fall, and was followed by rain that continued till three. At twelve, thermometer at 62°. At sun-set rained again ; thermometer 43°. About midnight the rain ceased.

August 11th.—Thermometer 42°. March at 9¼, over a plain which is very poachy. Our yaks, though very strong, labour through the soft ground, into which they frequently sink up to their bellies, but if left alone, would feed and wade along. *English* oxen would be much distressed and frightened in such quaggy soil. A hailstorm induces us to halt at 9825 paces, near a small river, at three o'clock. Thermometer, Even. 49°. *Cailas* mountain is supposed to be the favourite residence of Mahadeva and is situated opposite to the great lake of *Rawanhrad*, and little distant from that of *Mansarowar*. As its summit is always clothed with snow, it is but a cool seat ; however, this cold is said to be necessary, on account of the poison which has heated his frame ever since he swallowed it at the period of the *Sankh Avatar*.

August 12th.—Thermometer 40°. A party of people, having in charge a body of about seventy yaks loaded with *Awa jow*, in sacks, passed our encampment in the direction which we mean to take. March at 8¾. At 2400 paces, many wild asses, and some animals, which are thought more like mules than either horses or asses. At 6780 *Gangri* valley ends. The declivity goes to the left and the water of this land falls into the *Tirtapuri* river. At 7000, meet the old road. At 12,969, reach our ground opposite to our former encampment.

August 13th.—Thermometer 37°. March at 9.15. At 3970 paces fall into the *Misar* road. At 4460 descend to the bed of a rapid river, which we pass over a *Sankho.* Here we found many *Gelum* families of *Tatar* shepherds, who had been carrying to *Mansarowar* the ashes of their deceased relatives. At 5315 paces descend to another river, in rapidity and volume of current similar to the former. As there was here a *Sankho* three feet in breadth, we thought it right to attempt to force our yaks overloaded, but they disliked going on account of the height of the planks from the water, and the roaring of the river as it descended through the contracted channel. One, which was closely pressed, preferred leaping into the water from a bank of stones seven feet high, and swam under the bridge to the opposite side loaded. At 14,886 paces reach *Tirtapuri.* Wait in the veranda of the temple, where our wool is packed, until the arrival of our cattle with the baggage, which did not take place till near seven in the evening. Went into the temple to hear the *Gelums* repeat their vespers, the recital of which was accompanied with cymbals, and the beating of a deeptoned drum. The performance of the ceremony was preceded by the blowing of conches from the top of the temple. We generally found the *Gelums* assisted by the *Juaris* or *Dharmis.* One of these men said that the breach of chastity in a nun was compensated by a fine of fifty rupees, and that of a monk or *Gelum* by one of sixty.

August 14th—Halt at *Tirtapuri.* Thermometer 38°. A report is current amongst the *Juaris* and *Dharmis,* that the *Gorkhali* governor of *Srinagar* has written that he understands two *Europeans* have gone by the *Niti,* and two others by the *Dharma* pass, into the *Undes.* He desires information may be conveyed to him, as to who they are and with what intention they are going.

Some *Juaris* whom we here met, were concerned in the transaction respecting conveying shawl wool to *Belebre* fair for Mr. Gillman, which had excited the attention of the *Latakhis,* caused their complaint to the *Garpan,* and his severe edict against the clandestine sale of this article. One man told me that he had been seized by Ahmed Khan the *Latakhi,* for having a small quantity in his possession, which he said he was about to make into *pankhis.* This day I was much indisposed with fever.

August 15th.—Thermometer 44°. March at 9.30 : at 4700 paces come to an ascent of high Table Land. At 5836, a large river, supposed to issue from *Rawanhrad,* joins the *Terat* river, at S. 30 E. distant 1¼ mile, the little stream falls into it here likewise. The stream resulting from this junction now takes the name of the *Satudra.* At 6325 arrive at some mud temples with many caves in the rocks, shewing the place to have been once a winter resort of the *Uniyas,* but now deserted. A violent storm of wind, thunder, lightning, hail and rain, now sets in and lasts till nearly an hour. Rains again at sun-set. Thermometer 59°. Find two *Juaris* encamped here on the road to *Kien-lung* : one of these traders reproached us with spoiling their market, by selling our goods at too low a rate. The *Juaris* have hitherto been the principal medium through which the *Uniyas* have received, since the conquest of the hills by the *Gorkhalis,* the produce of *Hindustan* and *European* merchandise; and they have sold their wares at so high a rate, as to have confined the demand to a few rich individuals, such as the *Garpan, Debas,* and *Nerbas.*

August 16th.—Thermometer 45°. March at 8.30. River remaining close to the left. The low warm swampy land in the vales about *Tirtapuri* gives a grass which is cut and carried as hay for winter provision, for the horses of the *Garpan* and the people of *Kien lung, Daba* and *Dumpu.* The grain called *Awa-jau* raised in *Tikla-kote* is also given to them during the rigorous season, and said to be hearty food. As this grain grows in a rigorous climate, it is worth while to send some to *Britain* for the use of the inhabitants of the western isles.

At 5280 paces, reach a steep rocky pass of a stone laminated, rolled and whirled as at *Tirtapuri,* and apparently bound by the same agency. At 5600, broken ground presents appearances similar to those in which gold dust is found. At 5740, immense masses of broken rock of a brown colour, much veined with quartz, in the cavities of which is much rock crystal; that, which is small, generally transparent and regular in form; the large crystals ordinarily discoloured, full of flaws and fractured or shivered. At 6737, water drips over an inclined plain of rock and tastes salt and nauseous. At 7178, hot-water flows from the rock and covers the edges of its course with stony concretion of a yellowish colour. At 9465, reach a good *sankho* over the *Setlej* about fifteen paces long and four feet broad. On the right bank a natural fountain throws hot water a foot above its level, the edges of which are covered with a compact, hard, white, tufa, at a distance looking like ice. Come to our ground at 4.10 ; wait in a cave till our baggage arrives. Have this day come 9765 paces and encamp in a hollow surrounded by rocks formed by hot-water, opposite to the town of *Kien-lung*, situated on spires of rock on the right bank of the *Setlej* distant ¾ of a mile. The road of today has been of a very rugged description and the yaks with the wool and baggage were obliged to make a circuitous route over the tops of the hills, in order to prevent the loads being knocked off by the stones which projected from the sides of the path that we took. Yet, notwithstanding, many of the loads fell and at night it was discovered that the sirkar's bundle was missing, along with a small packet of *Cashmir* saffron which I had bought from the *Latakhi* agent.

The whole of the country, from *Tirtapuri* to *Kien-lung* or *Chinglung*, exhibits abundant proof of the presence of minerals and the rocks teem with springs of hot-water, impregnated with various mineral and saline substances, which we had neither leisure nor means to analyze : the springs of *Tirtapuri* seem charged with calcareous matter alone, which in process of time becomes lime-stone, marble, and calcareous spar. Near *Kien-lung*, the hot-water contains calcareous matter mixed with salts. Still nearer to this town, it is charged with iron and opposite to *Kien-lung* is a cavern into which drips water highly charged with sulphuric acid. This cavern is about twelve feet in breadth, at its mouth five feet high and about fourteen feet in depth, from the entrance to the back part. The floor consists of projections of calcareous matter mixed with sulphur, and cavities or pools of water about four feet deep, transparent, highly charged with sulphur. Hot sulphureous vapour issues through numerous holes in the floor and a person is thrown into perspiration almost immediately, without his breathing being incommoded, by the sulphur steam, provided he stands upright; but he is seized with coughing and a sense of suffocation, if he crouch on the floor, as happened to a *Hindu* who sat down. This occurs likewise in the grotto *dei cani*, and arises merely from the specific gravity of the sulphureous gas being greater than that of the atmospheric air, with which it does not mix with celerity. The sides of the cavern were formed by calcareous matter, and flour of sulphur, in some places straw colour, in others of a deep brimstone hue. The proportion of brimstone to the other material is nearly two to one. The side is so soft that it may be scooped off by the hand, and is a little moist. It is rubbed into powder with ease, and then mixed with oil which unites with the sulphur, and the calcareous matter subsides. Coal has not yet been found by the natives and fuel is only afforded by the furze in small quantity. If fuel were plentiful, I apprehend, that many hundreds of tons of sulphur might be obtained from this cavern and the immediately surrounding calcareous rock ; which even where white, is highly charged with sulphur. Immediately in front of the mouth of the cavern, and forming as it were its threshold, is a mound of calcareous stone, through chinks of which spring many jets of hot-water perfectly transparent, and of a smell and taste very similar to that of *Harrowgate*. The vast walls and masses of rock, which have been formed by the action of hot springs in this neighbourhood, shew an antiquity that baffles research and would afford food for sceptics.

The town of *Kien-lung*, consisting of about a hundred small houses, built of unburnt bricks painted grey and red, is situated upon the summit of a cluster of spires or natural pillars of indurated clay in the face of high banks of the same material, which overtop it by at least a hundred feet, whilst the town itself is at least 200 feet above the bed of the river, and in a retiring angle. This kind of situation seems particularly affected by the *Unias* for their winter retirements, and the preference is founded upon judicious principles ; for, from the conical shape of the pinnacles which form the foundation of the houses, the snow slips from them and falls into the valley below ; the height of the rocks behind guards them from the force of the winds which sweep over the summits of the hills and the elevation of the town above the level of the plain prevents the inhabitants from feeling the blasts which frequently rush along the course of the river with a violence which can scarcely be conceived. At present, from this being the season most favourable for pasturage, the greatest part of the inhabitants have left the town and gone to a distance with their flocks and herds.

August 17th.—Thermometer 42°. Four men were dispatched before day-break in search of the sirkar's bundle which they found, and returned by nine o'clock ; however, as the servants had begun to cook their victuals, we could not march till 1.50. The heat was very great. At 500 paces a strong sulphureous smell issues from hot springs ; the rocks stained yellow with sulphur, which appears in considerable quantity mixed with earth, in interstices betwixt masses of rock. At 2875, the channel of the river, from being broad, suddenly reduced to 50 yards : road along its edge stony. Reached our ground at seven P.M., 8383 paces. This has been one of the most rugged marches we have had in the *Undes.* As it grew dark, we fired carbines occasionally to apprise our people behind the direction we were encamped in, and at half past nine had the satisfaction to see them arrive without having met with any serious accident.

August 18th—.Thermometer 37°. March at 8.55. Some of the yak cows left the watercourse and went up the rock, the face of which became steeper as they advanced. One of them, finding herself separated from the great mass of her companions, without hesitation leaped from a height of about fourteen feet into the dry watercourse, apparently without being hurt by the shock and her example was followed by those which had taken the same path.

At 6900 paces, commence descending to a river formed of two branches, the right coming from S. 5 W. the left S. 35 W. They run N. 30 E. At 7625 reach the point at which the streams just mentioned join and breaking through a high mountain, fall into the *Setlej.* The bank on this side is as it were dissected ; the softer parts having been washed from the harder strata : the latter present a very irregular and extraordinary projecting surface. At 7700, cross the river 1½ feet deep ; 8000 descend to the second river, the water of which is more clear, and its banks afford more grass and furze for fuel. At 8050, cross and encamp at 1. P.M. Here we observed on the banks of the river many *larva* of a kind of locust which breeds on the stony plains of *Tatary*, marked on the body with a yellow ring on a black ground, and having a large horn in the tail. Two species of locusts breed here : one with purple wings by clapping the horny cases strongly together, it makes a smart crack as it flies. The other is twice as large, the carcass and wings of a yellow, spotted with points a little darker.

High wind from the *Himachal*, which lasted from three to nightfall. Thermometer at seven P.M. 56°

August 19th.—Slight frost. Thermometer 37°. March at 7. At 1300 paces, observe that the two rivers which we crossed yesterday join due east about 900 yards. At 5000 commence ascending the gorge and reach the summit of height which shuts the valley. At 5240, arrive at a pile of stones and descend by a tolerably good road, on which were many small fragments of different coloured jasper and white agate ; to the right is the river formed by two streams and now running parallel to our line of march about 2½ miles distant. At 15.700 commence descending ; the town of *Dumpu* in sight. This is built on a steep eminence forming part of a ridge stretching from the side of a mountain and sloping to a river, but rising at least 300 feet above the bed of the latter. Some ruined buildings on another eminence are separated from the town by a deep glen, in which runs a stream of delicious water. The banks of this watercourse cut into steps or narrow beds, are now covered by the grain called *Awa jau* now in ear, and watered by cuts from the stream begun near its source. The relief afforded to the eye by dwelling upon this, after having been so long tired with the repetition of bare rocks and of plains most scantily sprinkled with verdure, is such as cannot be conceived except by those who chance to have been in such situations. The inhabitants have also been equally industrious in turning to account a shelf of gently-sloping land at the foot of the ridge watered by the large river. The regularity and luxuriance of the crop shew that the soil would be very grateful if the farmer would irrigate sufficiently.

August 20th.—Halt at *Dumpu.* Thermometer 49.° The warmest day we have had since our arrival on the *Undes.* Amer Singh arrived at ten this morning. It appears that a dawk or post carried by horses, regularly goes from *Ghertope* to *Ouchong* (*Lassa.*) Each horse performs twenty kos a day and the journey takes up twenty two days at this rate. So that, giving the kos as two miles, the distance may be estimated at 880 miles. The intermediate country is most thinly peopled. The shawl goats are from *Latakh* to *Lassa,* where it is said there are sheep with finer wool than here. The *Ouchong* merchants buy woollen cloth at *Ghertope* from the *Latakhi* and *Juari* traders.

This day has been hot, with the exception of about half an hour, during which we had a smart shower of hail. Thermometer at night 56°. We were obliged to halt this day on account of our cattle being much tired, not only from the continued marching that they have had but from their having seldom been able to fill their bellies on account of the scarcity of grass in the course of our route.

August 21st.—Thermometer 45°. Leave *Dumpu* at 8.50. At 380 paces cross a small river, the water from which is made use of for irrigating some steps of land sown with *Awa-jau.* At 6514 reach Table Land ; a house of unburnt bricks about eighty yards to the left ; to the S. four or five others, which constitute the village of *Gengoul,* formerly tolerably populous, but now nearly deserted. It bears S. 60 W. from our encampment at 6740, at which we arrived at two P.M. The furze adjoining the *Awa-jau* fields, with some springy land, formed a favourite resort to hares and many *Chakarso* were heard in the neighbouring hills, and taking our guns, Mr. H. and myself had good sport. Found a partridge very like that of *England* in plumage and size, but which had a strange grunting call. This bird ran astonishingly swift, and I could not make it take wing. The *Chakors* breed in the hills and afforded excellent diversion, although at the same time it was very laborious and not without danger. This day three of our loaded

---

* Perdix rufa.

yaks fell over a steep bank from thirty to forty feet high into a ravine and, although they had struggled much to disentangle themselves, lay on their backs unable to get up on the ropes being cut, they rose apparently with very little injury. Thermometer at night 55°.

August 22nd.—Thermometer 37°. March at 8.45. At 11,900 paces arrive at a pile of stones with religious inscriptions carved upon them. *Deba* looks larger from hence than from the approach to it on the *Niti* road. We were welcomed by a crowd or half-naked, dirty, ragged children, in terms of friendship, and they were made happy for the moment by a few scraps of broken biscuit and some raisins. We proceeded to our original encampment in the town, having completed 12,575 paces at 4.40 P.M. We thought it proper to inform the *Wazir* and *Deba* of our arrival and to inquire where it would be agreeable to them that we should pay them a visit ; to this a reply was sent that they should be glad to see us the following morning. About half-past eight in the evening, the old *pundit* came to say that the moon was eclipsed, and we immediately heard the sound of trumpets and beating of drums and gongs from the temple of Narayan, and that erected on the site of the old palace of the Surjabanks Raja. This I presume was intended to drive away the dragon which during the time of an eclipse, is supposed by the *Chinese* to attempt to devour the moon. This eclipse was a total one ; but the obscurity was much less dense than I ever before observed it. Thermometer at night 55°.

August 23rd.—Halt at *Daba* or as pronounced, *Dhapa.* Thermometer 40° at sun-rise. At nine, a messenger from the *Wazir* and *Deba* stated that they were ready to receive us. In an apartment on the roof of the government house, we found the *Wazir* and *Deba,* along with the brother of the *Garpan,* and a person whom we took for a commander of cavalry, seated in an open verandah, in front of which we placed ourselves on a cushion. The presents made this time were less costly than those on our first interview with the young *Wazir* and *Deba.* After the usual complimentary inquiries, the *Garpan's* brother remarked that our journey had taken up a considerable time, and that he feared if our return to *Hindustan* were much longer delayed, it might be stopped altogether by a sudden fall of snow filling all the passes ; a circumstance not unusual at this season of the year. In answer to his remark, it was observed that we had been somewhat delayed by an illness which attacked me soon after I left *Ghertope* and that our cattle had been so reduced by continued marching and scanty supply of food, as to be incapable of proceeding as quickly as we wished. That we were very solicitous to return to our homes and should depart as soon as our cattle should be a little recruited, and the *Wazir* and *Deba* would assist us by hiring cattle to enable us to carry our wool to *Niti*. This later they promised to do without delay. I exchanged a knife with the *Wazir* for a curved horn snuff-box. After a sitting of two hours, during which a plate of raisins was placed before us, we took leave and made a visit to the *Lama*. The old man was apparently much pleased to see us and had tea prepared, of which according to our *Hindu* character we could not partake. Mr. H. brought as much orange cloth as would make him a dress, but this he refused, saying the weight of the obligation would be too great, it being out of his power to make a suitable return for such civility. I found that a knife and pair of scissors would be acceptable to him and I sent for them. He was most highly gratified by this token of regard, and gave us some slips of gauze sent to him by the *Deba Lama*, along with some red comfits made of flour, water and some red colouring matter; they were insipid, but having been made by the holy hands of the head of the church of this country, were said to possess extraordinary virtues, provided they were eaten before any other thing in the morning. These properties lay in a very small space for the comfits were no bigger than partridge shot. Being desirous of bringing a specimen of the *Unia* writing, some of which had appeared to me very neat, I requested that he would give me a written paper, as also one that had been printed. In compliance with my desire he gave me three slips of blue paper, on which some prayers were written in letters of gold by a *Gelum* lately dead, and with his own hand he struck off from a wooden block another prayer on a piece of coarse *Litbarua* paper. In the latter, having placed a few grains of *Awa-jau,* he blessed it and wrapping it round with an orange-coloured silk thread drawn out of an open stuff with loose ends apparently for this purpose, he recommended us to hang it in a particular direction, and we should find it in some respects useful to us. He caused some tea-leaves in a mass to be brought to us, along with a small piece of soda, which in this country is always employed to extract more of the colouring matter and flavour of the tea than would be done by the water alone which is here hard. A cheese made of meal and milk slightly daubed over with coarse sugar and having a few raisins stuck in it, with a cake of a sweetmeat made of sugar and butter, and a large plate of raisins formed his present. The cheese had a very strong smell, and as well as the tea and sweetmeat was given to our servants. The old man finding that we would not take back the cloth, requested that it might be given him the following day in the presence of the *Gelums.* The more we have seen of this priest, the more we are pleased with the simplicity of his manners and the liberality of his sentiments as far as the stupidity of our interpreter would give us to understand his conversation.

In the evening we were desired again to visit the *Wazir* and *Deba.* They were engaged in writing to the *Garpan* ; and we requested that a letter, in general terms, informing him of our safe arrival and expressing our thanks for his attentions, might be transmitted to him in our name, which was done. It was promised that on the following morning some cattle should be brought, that we might select two for our own riding at the rate of fifteen rupees nominal per head, and that others would be furnished to carry our wool and baggage. Two trays, containing rice with a lump of butter, secured in a piece of the skin of a yak with the hair on, were put before us as a present, along with a plate of raisins, and a written order, signed by the *Wazir* and *Daba,* for five goats, was directed to be given to the steward, who would on receiving it immediately forward the animals. Thermometer 55° in the evening. At night the *Wazir* sent an agate snuff-box, in exchange for that of horn. After I had the latter in my possession, I observed a small ring of gold, by means of which the bottom was capable of being taken out in order that the snuff may be put in, the mouth being too small for this purpose. I could not help thinking, that the *Wazir* had overlooked this circumstance in the first instance, and now recollecting it, thought he had made a bad bargain. Under this impression, and resolving to defeat his avarice in this matter, I pretended to misunderstand his message, and returned another knife with a small silver-capped glass salt muffineer that had been admired in the morning by him. The agate box was in the shape of an urn flattened at the sides, and surmounted at each shoulder by the mask of a satyr. This appears to me an antique of *Grecian* workmanship ; or, if it should be of *Tatar* fabric, the following does credit to their ingenuity. The *Wazir* seemed pleased with his new bargain.

August 24th.—Thermometer 39°. This morning we went to the lodging of a *Latakhi-Cashmirian* merchant, who shewed us *Russian* leather and *French* woollen cloth. The *Latakhi* said, that the *Russians* had latterly imported much merchandise into this part of *Tatary* through *Yarkund*, which is forty days' journey from *Latakh* and fifteen from *Bokhara*.

At night the *Wazir* and the rest of his council sent for the old pandit, and the brother of the *Garpan* said, that they were anxious for our departure, left some accident might occur to us, which would be a source of great uneasiness to them. That we had now passed through their country once ; and as we were *Firinghis*, we could not be allowed to come a second time. The pandit said, that they well knew he was conscious that they had it not in their power to prevent our visiting the country whenever we pleased. That whether we should do so or not depended upon the orders of our superiors ; but, if we should our dealings would always be governed by the same integrity which they had already witnessed and which they could not but approve. He then departed. This day a well looking *Juari* in a clean dress, of the name of Deb or Deba Singh, came to pay his respects to us, he was son to a man of consequence of the name of Dhamu, who had ordered him to come over, and, whether we were *Mahants* or not, to offer his services in whatever we thought he might be useful. If he thought us not *Mahants*, he was directed to say that 2000 men were ready to take arms for the cause of the *Raja* whenever a rallying point was furnished. He said, that, as our journey had been long, and we had, he understood, been made to incur unnecessary expense, he should be happy to furnish a draft on *Srinagar* for a thousand rupees, if it would afford us any accommodation, and would take the amount at *Haridwar*, either in goods or money, as might be most agreeable to us. We thanked him for the offer ; which he declined, but employed him in some little offices in which he was serviceable. I sold the whole of the coral beads I had provided, for ninety rupees, to Amar Singh, who passed them over to Deb Singh for fifty shawl-wool goats and twenty sheep, to be delivered to him at *Niti*, and to be brought down to *Chilkia* by Harkh Deb. This, though much under their value, was the best return I could form, as, in the event of accident to our first batch of goats, the second might fill their place ; and this precaution was the more necessary, as all the persons we met with, said, that by far the greater part of these animals, if taken through the hills before the cold weather should have set in, would die on the march.

August 25th.—Thermometer 41°. The *Wazir* and *Deba* sent word, that the yaks would be ready to take our loads this morning ; we returned an answer, that we should not be able to march until the following morning : and that this would depend upon their performing their contract. A messenger returned with twelve rupees from the *Wazir* and *Deba*, instead of a like number of goats which they had undertaken to supply, but now said they could not furnish ; and this was soon followed by those persons who said that the people from *Ghertope* were extremely anxious to return, and expected we would set off this morning, as they could not depart until we had began our march. We repeated our arguments and ordered our cattle out of the town to graze. An order was given by the *Wazir*, etc. to shut the gates, and we sent two resolute men to open it, and to turn out the yaks. This they effected without resistance. We then remonstrated in very strong terms with the

Wazir and *Deba* on the impropriety, and meanness of their conduct, after a little conversation they both appeared ashamed and said they did not act from themselves, but under the authority of the *Ghertope* messengers by order from the *Garpan*. Immediately after the *Wazir* and *Deba* returned, these people learnt our intention, and without waiting for our visit, saddled their horses and went off. The *Wazir* and *Deba*, sent word privately, that, if we would take saffron, they would in the evening take some of our cloth. The *Latakhi* saffron is received by the *Latakhis* from the *Cashmirian* traders, in payment for the shawl wool furnished by the latter ; and again given to the *Unias* in payment for the wool taken from them. It appears to me pure, but dear ; however, the highness of price is, in some measure, owing to the form of the transaction being by barter. According to our promise we went to the government house, where we were received with a cordiality calculated to efface the impression of the late transactions, and which our conduct on the occasion shewed had produced that effect. The *Wazir* and *Deba* said, that really there was much danger of our entering *Hindustan* being prevented altogether, if our departure were delayed ; that if they followed their own inclination, they could wish us to stay longer ; but the season was advanced, and it would much grieve both the *Garpan* and themselves if any accident were to occur to us.

August 26th.—Thermometer 37°. We commenced our march from *Deba* at ten A.M., following the direction by which we arrived at first, in which line we continued, and crossing the *Tiltil* reached the junction of the two streams before mentioned at twelve, having come only about three miles. Here the measurement commenced as we took a new road. At 2.30 took up our ground for encampment. Our baggage did not reach us till eight at night, in consequence of many of the loads falling off, from the ruggedness of part of the road, and from our people having kept in the direction of the former line instead of following us exactly. The road we have now taken is in the straight line for *Niti*, the other was circuitous, but better. Deb Singh came in the evening, and promised to send us three fat sheep for our consumption on the road. When the sun set it became very cold ; before sun-set thermometer 48°.

August 27th.—As our cattle had been much reduced by their long journey from *Ghertope* to *Mansarowar* and back to *Deba*, they had performed their work of yesterday but weakly, and it was therefore judged advisable to halt, that they might have a chance of filling their bellies, although the pasturage was even here but scanty. Deb Singh was very anxious to receive a certificate of his endeavours to be useful, and a recommendation that he should be permitted to enter the Company's provinces paying only the usual duties. The papers required by Deb Singh were given to him, and he took his leave highly satisfied in appearance. Much ice in the river this morning.

August 28th.—Hard frost. In some places the ice was 2 1/2 inches thick. Thermometer 28°. Marched at 9. At 7300 paces reach our ground, and encamp at 12.30. Thermometer in the open air 67°. Found many ammonites in iron-stone, generally broken. Much iron in the mountains, which have scarcely any vegetable upon them, and are rapidly frittering into fragments. We are now about one third of the *Ghati* which separates *Hindustan* from *Tatary*. Mountains are less high and bold than those farther on in *Butan*. Two yaks have been left behind from fatigue, although the march has not been long, yet parts have been very distressing. The rivulet or rather river for when it fills its channel it well deserves this name, is called *Chang-lu*. It is formed by three or four branches, which issue from the heights below the *Niti Ghati*, and it disembogues itself into the *Setlej*.

August 29th.—Thermometer 19°. Hard frost ; and very cold to our feelings. Leave our ground at ten A.M. At 3745 paces reach the bed of the river near which we halted on the first day, after crossing the *Ghati*, in our road to *Daba*. The name of this is *Jandu*. It rises N 85 W., and runs N. 80 E. to the *Setlej*. The banks are formed by stupendously lofty mountains. At 6125 reach the *Ghati*, which separates *Butan* from the *Undes*, and which has upon it a large pile of stones, the offering of travellers, surmounted by rags in token of the victory they achieved in reaching so great a height. The *Ghati* is about half a mile broad, almost without any vegetable. The wind from the *Butan* mountains covered with snow is most piercingly cold. We turned out of the road, to the left hand, and, in order to save a little distance, scaled an ascent which cost us double in time. One of the yaks, which had fallen from a precipice a few days before, and received such a shock as rendered him unfit for carrying a load, after he had ascended a few steps, suddenly returned, and ran downwards towards the river as rapidly as the badness of the road would admit, and faster than any one who has never seen these animals travel over crags would suppose possible. I had got upon a *Jabu* (or mule between a yak and a cow), and was bringing up the rear. The animal charged me, and endeavoured to overthrow may steed, who however stood firm. Luckily he took my thigh between his horns, and did not hurt me materially. When he found room, he did not repeat the attack, but continued his course towards the river, upon the bank of which he stood still. I leaped off the *Jabu*, had him secured, and passed a cord through a hole in his nose. Though one of the most tractable animals I had ever seen, before the fall, he now was become wholly the reverse ; I saw, that some derangement of the brain had taken place, and was obliged to abandon him. Another yak, the best of my herd, actually separated the hoofs from the toes of the hind feet in exertions to climb the stones ; and after bleeding very largely and prosecuting his journey in great pain, when a stop was made to allow of the others taking breath, he also refused to proceed. The *Unias*, who had brought the wool on hire, on the *Wazir* and *Deba's* cattle, sat down every five or six steps on stones, and smoked and spum yarn till the animals were disposed to proceed. This was a terrible day. The descent was very slippery as well as steep, and required great precaution. The ascent of the *Gahti* measured 2110 paces, the descent 1750. At 9835 reach a good grassy plain on the left bank of the rivulet, which runs from the *Ghati* to the south, in order to fall into the *Dauli* and encamp at 5.50. The goats reaching the bottom of the *Ghati* first, instead of taking the right road, by the carelessness of the people in charge, went up a crag about

500 feet above the level of the road, and very leisurely placed themselves on the very edge of the precipice ; a mountaineer, native of *Kamaun* followed them, and by throwing stones and calling, at length succeeded in dislodging them from the dangerous post they had taken. The latter rank, in coming down, deranged loose stones which tumbled down an abrupt slope, by which they descended with a force that threatened to overthrow those which were nearest the bottom ; and it really was entertaining to see with what address, whilst at a run, they avoided the blows of the rolling stones without turning their heads in the direction of their descent. In this march we met with much wild *Chana*, not yet ripe. This might be an acquisition to the mountains of *Scotland* and *Wales*. Thermometer at night 39°, wind high

August 30th.—Snow falling on the adjacent monutains, and in less quantity on our tents ; thermometer 37°. Had we not crossed the *Ghati* yesterday, we should have found it difficult to-day. As the pasturage here was good, and it is a long time since our cattle have fairly filled their bellies, we halted this day. In the course of the morning the *Unias* in charge of the *Wazir's* sheep came up, and stated that they could not bring up our cattle : that at the foot of the dry watercourse being unwilling to move, and the other very lame. Thermometer at night 41°.

August 31st.—Thermometer 41°. Water frozen during the night. Frost greatest just before sun-rise. March at eight A.M. At 1280 paces arrive at the bed of the *Dauli* river. The stream is now much broader and deeper than when we crossed before. The rivulet, near which we encamped last night, falls into the *Dauli* here, which is about two feet deep and very rapid. The descent was very rugged, and winding amidst large blocks of stone : much of the *Chana* on both the banks of the river ; the grains smaller than that cultivated ; but the plant throws out many pods, much foliage, and appears hardy. At 3700 paces reach the ground on which we encamped in going ; and, finding our cattle much fatigued from the badness of the road, abandon our intention of endeavouring to reach *Gotang*. When we went to the *Undes*, the mountains, by which we are now surrounded, were almost entirely bare ; they are now covered with verdure ; and many of the plants going to seed. The white, yellow, and red flowering strawberry have bore abundance of flowers, but only a cone of seed without any pulp. Whether in a more kindly soil, they would produce fruit may be worth trying.

5

JOURNEY TO LAKE MANSAROVAR : SEPTEMBER

September 1st.—Thermometer 36°. March at eight by the same route we came. Descend the steep *Ghati* to the bed of the *Dauli.* One of the yaks could not be driven round the projection of rock which led to it, but resolutely charged back again in spite of sticks and stones. The *Unias* went by a lower road along the steep face of the rock. The stream of the *Dauli* was very rapid and reached half way up the yak's shoulder. After having gone about a hundred yards, perpendicular rocks, dipping into the river, compelled them to cross again to the right bank, and a third crossing took place immediately above the *Sanga,* which was so bad that our men were afraid of going along it even with very light loads. Their apprehensions were reasonable enough, for the *Sanga* was made only of two loose sticks of fir, with large loose stones sloped nearly in the angle of 45°. At 6100 paces, the *Dauli* meets the stream which comes from behind the *Nar-Narayan Parbat* near *Bhadrinath.* This river is larger than the *Dauli.* Of the two arches of snow, which lay over the river as we passed before, one had dissolved, and nothing remained but the abutments ; the other was entire and still of great thickness. The road was almost as bad as possible. Indeed it is scarcely in the power of imagination to suppose, that such a surface could be trodden by men and cattle, without their being precipitated into the *Dauli*, which rolled a tremendous current at the foot of the slope, over which the path run (if that could be with any propriety called such a name, when effaced in many places by recent slips, and in others by blocks of stones, for nearly a quarter of a mile together.) This was a march of disaster. The yaks, in inclining their bodies towards the mountain to prevent their slipping into the river, struck their loads against portions of rock, and tore the packages. At every hundred yards, there was a cry of something being wrong. The people anxious to get over the dangers and difficulties of the march, in opposition to what I could say, persisted in driving the cattle too fast. The day was very hot ; and the yaks, oppressed by the heat, the weight of their burthens, and the incessant calling and flinging of stones, found no more effectual way of escaping from these annoyances, than by running down the almost perpendicular face of the rock and dashing into the cold stream. Sometimes by the slipping of the soil they fell into the water with some violence, and after cooling themselves, to my great mortification, generally lost their loads in climbing over stones to regain the road. At 3, reached our ground ; and in the evening, I had the mortification to learn, that two yaks in the last detachment could not be brought forward. One had slipped into a niche in the bank of the river and could not get up ; and the other had become so very lame, as to be unable to pass over the sharp edged blocks of stone which lay in the road. At night thermometer 56°.

September 2nd.—Halt at *Gotang*. Thermometer 56°. At night. 54°.

September 3rd.—Thermometer 44°. March at 10, A.M. The sight of trees is extremely pleasing after our being so long absent from them. The rhubarb had now run to seed. I cut up many roots, but found the whole more or less spongy and rotten. From the holes I have seen in the *Turkey* rhubarb, and its irregular knobby form I apprehend that this is its usual habit, Gentian is met with in great abundance, is called here

Catci, and given in infusion to goats and sheep ; most especially, when, in travelling towards *Hindustan*, they are supposed to be distressed by heat. The woods here are composed of birch, the great *Rhododendron*[1], willow[2], and mountain-ash with brown berries. The road was extremely bad ; and the trouble we had from the falling off of the loads, and from our yak cows and calves straying up the mountains, and down the sides of stupendous precipices, where it was scarcely possible for them to fix one claw, is not to be conceived. It was nearly night when I reached *Niti*, notwithstanding Amer Singh brought several yaks to assist us. The lame yak was brought to *Gotang*, and there left to recruit in the abundant pasture of that place ; that, which had fallen into a nook of rock near the river, could not be found. The upper part of *Butan* is now suffering much from scarcity of grain, in consequence of the *Juaris* and *Dharmis* plundering the *Gangaris*, or people living on the banks of the *Ganges* within the hills, who were in the habit of bringing up the grain they raised, and that which they procured from below.

September 4th.—Thermometer 54° in the morning ; 80° at noon. In the afternoon there was a fall of rain, accompanied by thunder. At night thermometer 54°. The gooseberry-bushes, which were in flower when we were here before, are now full of fruit, of which only a few are ripe. They are, as I conjectured, of the burgundy kind, but small ; and the pulp is much smaller than that of *England* in proportion to the bulk of the seed ; but this may be remedied by cultivation. Of currants I found two varieties, one orange-coloured with small fruit in small clusters, the other of a dark purple or rather nearly black in large bunches from a tree, with bark like that of the black currant in *England*, but with the flavour of the red one, only more acid. This morning we sent to announce to the *Seyanas* that we had arrived, were anxious to depart, and were in want of provisions. In the evening Arjun and Gujaa came, and said that the terms of carrying the baggage should be adjusted tomorrow.

1. Rhododendron puniceum. *Rox*
2. Salix tetrasperma. *Rox.*

September 5th.—Thermometer 48°. At night 62°.

September 6th.—Morning cloudy with small rain ; thermometer 52°. At night 54°.

September 7th.—A party of *Garkhali Sipahis,* consisting of a havildar and four privates, arrived today for money due from the *Nitias* to their company under the command of Bhacti Thapa. The havildar brought a letter from Bhawani Singh, ordering the *Niti* people to render every assistance in their power to us ; and that, if they should not do so he would levy a heavy fine upon them. The havildar came to pay his respects to us, and said, that he had received directions to pay every attention to us in his power, and that he should immediately procure carries. We gave him five rupees in *Timashas,* as an earnest of what he might expect if he exerted himself. He promised, that we should start tomorrow. In about an hour he returned with three other *Sipahis,* and twenty rupees were tendered to him as subsistence money to the carriers. He refused this at first, saying that our effects were to be conveyed free of expense to *Joshi Math.* This we declined, saying it was improper for people coming on objects of *Dharm* (piety), to have baggage carried without hire : and he took the money.

September 8th.—At 12.30 we began our march. At 3200 paces reach *Gamsali,* whenee the people took up our loads immediately. At 3315 cross the *Sankha* of the rivulet from the right, now much swollen. At 4182 reach *Bampa.* Here the loads were again carried on towards *Pharkia* ; and at 4886 paces encamp to the north of our former ground near the village, at 4° 55. Wind high and some rain. The crops of *Phaphar,* buck wheat, are very good. These with the *Awa-jou* are nearly ripe. Barberries are affording a second crop. The *Shikari,* who received from us two rupees on the banks of the *Chang-lu* for killing a *Baral,* was engaged at *Gamsali* watching the crops, and said he was debarred using his gun by the *Seyanas* until the crops were got in, as snow would certainly follow the explosion. We respected their prejudices, and did not go out, although the black partridge tempted us to do so, in pursuit of them, by their frequent calls.

September 9th.—Thermometer 50°. Marched at 11. The

villagers of *Pharkiah* made much hesitation in taking up our loads, notwithstanding the *Gorkhali* havildar threatened them with a fine, and offered a deduction of two rupees from their payment of revenue. At length they agreed, and a party set off. At 4900 paces cross the *Sankha* over the *Dauli*, at the place where a wall is built with a door in it for the purpose of preventing the goats and sheep laden with salt and wool coming from the *Undes* or northermost part of *Butan*, springing into the river. Whilst taking a little rest upon a stone. I heard the call of *Chakors* on some rocks of great height, to which I gained access by a steep, long, and difficult route. Whilst clambering up, I had very nearly placed my hands upon a brown snake which had got halt its body into a hole, before I was able to strike it. I succeeded in getting three *Chakors*, one of which was of great size, and had large double spurs, one above the other on each leg. At 4.35 reached *Malari*, having come 5740 paces. The crops of Millet, *Phaphar*, and *Awa-jou* look well. The bed of ice, which filled the bed of the *Malari* river, has disappeared, but the tops of the high mountains to the east are covered with snow.

September 10th.—Thermometer 54°. Rained till 11. Halted on account of our loads not having come up yesterday. As far as *Lata* southwards, the country is called *Buthant*, but it is understood that the *Rengni* river separates that country from *Hindustan*. The *Butias* pay a small sum of money annually to the *Unias*, or its value in kind ; and the quota of *Malari* is six rupees, which is commonly in barley. The inhabitants of the whole tract between *Lata* and *Niti* complain much of the extortions of the *Gorkiahs*. The poorest man is compelled to pay a poll tax of four *kacha* rupees. This has caused many villages to be deserted ; and the population is now much diminished. This evening whilst looking at our goats, *Malari* man came to us and entered into conversation. We asked how it happened that one portion of the village was in ruins, and that so many of the houses were in such a state of decay ; The former inhabitants, he said, were dead ; and when inquiry was made, if there had been any sudden and violent sickness, he answered, that, of the particular quarter to which we pointed, the tenants had been plundered of their goats by the *Juaris* ; that, unable without these animals to carry on their usual traffic of grain and salt with the *Unias*, they were deprived of the means of paying their rent to the *Gorkiahs*, who took the remainder of their cattle, their cooking utensils, the rings out of the noses of their wives and daughters, and seized their children as slaves. Many persons were actually starved to death, and others fled. Including the regular rent, he said, the inhabitants of *Malari* had an annual sum of 1000 rupees forced from it, although the first only amounts to 250. "In the time of our *Rajas*," said the man, "these yards, now empty, were filled with goats ; each old inhabitant had one house to place his son in when married, and another for his daughter, who had a portion in cattle. We were then, if not wealthy, at least at our ease, and occupied and happy. At present we are poor and wretched. If we had masters like you once again, these pens might contain the same number of cattle as formerly ; but at present, if a man by his industry raises a small stock of goats, a *Juari* or a *Dharmi* plunderer attacks him and carries them off, and we can get no redress from our present masters, nor are we strong enough to resist or make reprisals." Independently of the direct plunder they obtain without any other caution than putting a number of men under arms, the *Juaris* are interested in destroying the trade of the *Niti Ghati*, in order that they may have a larger proportion of the profitable traffic with the *Undes*. At night, the thermometer was 58°.

September 11th.—Thermometer 51°. March at seven by the route we came. At 3575 paces cross a *sankha* over the *Dauli* to the right bank. The descent from hence is very rapid, and the stream is much broken by vast fragments of rock and heaps of timber which have been much accumulated since our passing upwards. In one place the river has worked its way under a kind of arch formed of these materials. At 6240 paces reach the village of *Jhelim*, now in ruins with the exception of two or three houses. A villager said that sometime ago Deb Singh, our *Juari* acquaintance, swept the country during the space of two months, and carried off two thousand head of goats, sheep and neat cattle, without receiving any molestation from the *Gorkiahs*, or being compelled to make restitution or any kind of reparation.

September 12th.—Halt at *Jhelim*, as our loads did not come last night.

September 13th.—Thermometer 52°. March at seven and half, A. M. ; no tidings of the loads. The village of *Jhelim* is situate on the face of a hill considerably higher than the road from *Lata* to *Malari* ; descending therefore, we fell into the old route. On the road we were met by a messenger from Bhawani Singh Negi, with a letter from him, and another from Jagrup, jamadar of the party now at *Baragaon* and *Joshi Math*. The former stated, that the *Gorkiahs* had distressed him much on account of having assisted in forwarding our baggage ; that his life would have been forfeited had we not returned by this road ; but that now he was perfectly at ease, and disposed to do every thing in his power to serve us. Jagrup said, that he would take care that we should have every facility that he could afford us in our return : Bhawani Singh stated, that we might take the *Pain Khandi*, or *Budan* road, as might be most agreeable. At 5645 paces cross the *Dauli* over a very bad *Sankho* to the left bank. Here the road, which is very bad, ascends rapidly ; in many places, little more than a foot broad ; and the projections from above oblige the passenger to creep under them almost immediately over the bed of the river, which is about 500 yards below. At 7025 paces reach the summit from whence the descent is very difficult and steep : indeed were a person from below to see travellers above, he could not fail of feeling much anxiety for their situation. At 7650 paces reach our former ground and encamp. A *Sankho* had been washed away, and the loss of a long tree, not worth three rupees in this country, endangers the loss of life to every one who attempts this most dangerous route, of which no conception can be formed by description. Let it suffice to say, that the very goats resisted attempting some parts of it for a considerable time ; and that we were in more than one place reduced to the necessity of creeping on our hands and knees : yet every one arrived without accident, and the *Jabu* climbed and descended in a manner that created admiration ; but in one spot it was thought advisable that he should attempt an almost perpendicular face of rock, rather than be obliged to come down by another so steep that it was a task of great danger for man. By a long detour he reached us over a tract known to our guides only, but the man who had the care of him declared, that this care was superfluous, for that he could come down a surface as steep as was practicable for man. He had been brought to the side of the river, under an idea that he might have crossed ; and from the height of the bank where I stood, I thought the attempt attended with little danger ; insomuch, that the best swimmer in the party having declined the task, I had resoved upon trying. However, on reaching the bed of the river and passing one stream, I was deterred from the experiment, in consequence of the force and velocity of the current, the extreme coldness of the water, and the danger of being dashed against the stones' or stumps of trees.

Although money had been given to the *Seyanas* of *Jhelim* for the hire of the carriers, they had kept the money, and not furnished a particle of food to the unfortunate people who had to bear the burden and heat of the day. The oppression exercised by the government renders natives equally oppressive in proportion to their power. Thermometer at night 62°.

September 14th.—Thermometer 58°. March at 9.25 along the left bank of the *Dauli* ; one of my finest goats, heavy with young and the boldest in the whole herd, fell into the stream and was hurried away by the current. The bridge was about twelve inches broad and formed by a fir-tree, a little flattened on its upper surface, and a round sapling on each side. Whilst the goats crowded at the foot of the *Sankho*, two went on boldly, but when they had reached within a few feet of the opposite side, the pressure of the feet of the goats had pushed forwards one of the side spars, and unluckily that on which a goat was ; one end fell down, and the other tilting up, threw the poor animal into the stream. This spot has brought me much disaster ; for it was on its bank, within twenty yards of the *Sankho*, that the pandit's slave dashed my watch from my girdle upon the stones. However this accident did not affect me, although seriously inconvenient, one-tenth so much as the loss of one poor goat that cost only a rupee : but this latter had been attained with more difficulty than the watch had cost me. At 8025 paces reached the road running under the village of *Tolma*, which, surrounded by fields of the crimson *marcha*, looks very pretty. The *marcha* is a plant which I mistook in my journey up-wards for the *lal-sag* of *Hindustan*, or the *Amaranthus Gangeticus* ; and the *Sipahis*, who had accompanied the party which went in 1808, to survey the *Ganges*, fell into the same error, and used it as a pot-herb. In a short time, those who had eaten much of it were affected with purging and soreness in the inside of the mouth. The natives of the hills, however, employ it without injury whilst it is young, but I neglected to inquire in what manner it was dressed. I thought we should be able to reach *Lata* this evening, and therefore pushed on. Having arrived at the foot of the mountain (which we ascended on leaving *Lata*) the sky became suddenly clouded, and large drops of rain, with gusts of wind, announced an approaching storm. As the day closed rapidly, I saw it would not be possible to pass over the rugged mountainous road without accident, as much of it lay on the edge of the cliff over the river, and therefore determined to take up my lodging for the night. A small cavity under a ledge of rock just sheltered me from the rain. Having stretched my carpet and blanket on the ground, I went to bed dinnerless ; and my companion fared no better. The principal part of our servants remained behind taking such lodging as they could find : but they were much better circumstanced than their masters, as they had their food along with them.

September 15th.—Thermometer 58°. At eight A.M. began our march. The town of *Lata*, consists only of eight or nine houses, and a temple of Nanda *Deba*, at which officiate some priestesses, who do not, according to report, either take a vow, or observe the practice, of chastity, being allowed what intercourse with the other sex they may think proper to take, without restraint. Jowahir Singh had now a knowledge of our real character, and said that he would fetch the loads from *Malari* as soon as he should have seen his brother. He was anxious to have a goat to sacrifice to the deity of the place in gratitude for our safe return ; but I believe that his own appetite had a greater share in inducing him to prefer this request, than any motive of religion. Jowahir says that provisions are very scarce, owing to the visitations of the locusts, with which the country has been plagued for the last two months. For the preceding two days we have seen many locusts directing their flight towards the *Undes*, where they breed. Thermometer at night 72°.

September 16th.—Thermometer 64°. March at 8. At 1340 paces we come to a *Sankho* over the river *Reni* which separates *Butan* from *Hindustan*, and falls into the *Dauli*. At 7542 encamp in the fields belonging to the village of *Dak*. Our dinner consisted of some pumpkin boiled with *dal*, and hunger made the dish palatable.

September 17th.—Thermometer 66°. March at 8 A.M., rain increases to such a degree as to prevent as enjoying the pleasure of the shade of the horse-cheanut and rhododendron trees under which we pass. In one of the former were monkeys feeding heartily on their fruit, which is relished by few animals. At 1140 paces reach the summit of the ascent ; and at 3145 reach a fountain, near which we encamp, on a spot of uncultivated ground surrounded by the *Sarson*, or mustard, in flower.

The *Nishanchi* or colour-bearer of a company belonging to Bhacti Thapa, paid us a visit. Afterwards Bhawani Singh Negi made his appearance. He says that our loads shall be brought from *Mallari* in a short time, and that he will charge the expense as a set-off against our account of 101 rupees advanced to him on his bond. Thermometer at night 64°.

September 18th.—Thermometer 62.° At noon 74° Night 64°. Many showers of short continuance but smart in the course of the day, with intervals of sun-shine and heat. The jamadar Jagrup sent some rice and flour last night, and to day a present of game.

This man was with Sheristha Thapa at *Srinagar* in 1808, when Mr. H. came with a party, to survey ; but on account of his disguise did not recognise him. He gave the following account of the transactions which had reached us in a confused manner, whilst in the *Undes*. Dasrath, who was formerly in power at *Srinagar*, but had been displaced, had written information to *Catmandu*, that Bhacti Thapa had allowed two *Europeans* to go through the country in his division into the *Undes.* The *Nepalese* government sent Bhacti a reprimand, on the receipt of which he sent Jagrup with thirty men to examine into the foundation of the reports propagated by Dasrath, with whom he had long been at enmity. On Jagrup reaching *Baragaon*, he found that Bhawani Singh had left his house to avoid the oppression of a party of Dasrath's men which to the amount of ninety had taken possession of his premises, broken open his granaries, and used the grain they had found in them. He had armed all his dependents : but on Jagrup sending him assurances of his personal safety, he went over to him. Bhawani then made a declaration of his ignorance of our being *Europeans*, and of his having received the sum of eighty-seven rupees to forward our baggage to *Niti.* Dasrath, in his letter to Bhacti, accused Bhawani Singh of having taken three thousand rupees, and made use of this falsehood, as a plea to ruin Bhawani by extorting that sum from him. The report forwarded to *Catmandu* stated, that we had gone with an intention of building two-forts, one at *Niti* and one in the *Undes*, to garrison them with *Marchas*, and thence proceed by *Bubesin* to join the *Sikhs*, with whose arms we proposed to invade the country. The accounts amongst the country people were ridiculous enough. One reported that a letter had arrived from *Delhi*, stating that we had stolen the philosopher's stone, and three lacks of rupees from the Company's wife.

A letter arrived from Bandhu Thapa's son, now at *Solur*, directing Jagrup to treat us with attention, and to take care that no part of our property should receive any injury. He was anxious, that we should march tomorrow to *Solur*, which is five kos below *Joshi-math.* To this the rainy state of the weather was objected : but it was promised that we would go as soon as the weather became fair. The motive he assigned for our going thither was, that we should be able to get provisions easily, which could not be done at *Baragaon.*

September 19th.—Thermometer 59°. During the night, the summits of the neighbouring mountains have been covered with a fall of snow. Halt at *Baragaon.* About 2 P.M. it began to rain smartly and continued without intermission until 6, leaving the air cold and disagreeably damp. After sun-set thermometer 16°.

September 20th.—Thermometer 57.° The jamadar having strongly represented that they could not procure provisions without the greatest difficulty at *Baragaon*, but that they should be able to get abundance at *Solur*, we agreed to march as far as *Joshi-math* today, provided it did not rain. At 11.15 we marched. At 1300 paces cross a watercourse from which the air before us was filled with an immense body of locusts, some of which were of a light yellow ; but the greater number of an organge colour. On heaps of weeds that were dry, and on stones, they assembled by forties and fifties and remained quiet in the sun-shine; but others were actively employed in eating the heads of *Mandua*[3] now nearly ripe. They had been here about two months, but had not done as much mischief as I should have supposed. A leopard made frequent visits to this neighbourhood, had taken away three children, and killed two men ; but the place to which he resorted with his prey was unknown. At the same place where we encamped before, we now pitched our tents, close to a temple. Every other spot for a great extent was occupied by crops of rice, *Marcha*, *Mandua* and *Sawah.*[4] The people of the neighbourhood said, that the leopard would certainly make an attack upon our goats in the night ; and we took precautions accordingly by setting a strong watch with loaded guns, and keeping up a good fire.

September 21st.—Thermometer 55°. The leopard has committed some ravage in a village to the East of *Joshi-math.* In this village my goats were yesterday entangled, and with no small trouble and loss of time I extricated them out of the filthy and intricate roads. Goats are cleanly animals : when they reached one filthy spot, the leading animals stopped, and the whole flock was delayed in a narrow path overhung with long grass, and from which issued a streak drawn upwards by the heat of the sun, that was scarcely supportable by man, and must have been greatly annoying to the animals shut up

---

3. Eleasion Coracana.
4. Panicum Colonum.

in an alley of this offensive vapour. At length they clambered up some large blocks of stones.

Our march did not take place till 2.15, owing to the *Gorkha* party having served themselves with carriers for their loads, before they gave any to us. On reaching the foot of the hill, half way up which are many detached cottages, which form the village of *Solur*, I found my flock, which had started at an early hour. We went up, and after an ascent of about a mile through narrow paths and fields of *Marcha*, *Sawa*, and *Sarson*, reached the residence of Bhawani Singh, at the close of day, where was a stone threshing-floor almost covered with hemp, on which we pitched our tents. Gave the body of a goat which died, to the *Gorkia Sipahis*, who requested to have it for their night's repast.

September 22nd. –Halt. Bhawani Singh has not come here according to his promise. We found Bandhu Thapa's son, the nephew of the general, Bhacti, sick of an intermittent.

September 23rd.—After breakfast we set off accompanied by a farmer, who said that he thought it likely we should find wild hogs, bears, deer, and pheasants, if we would go up to the top of a high wooded mountain to the left, which formed part of the great *Tugasi* range. We ascended a steep ridge and passed through a forest of fir, cedar, and cypress,[5] with sycamore, horse-chesnut, walnut and yew trees, the latter are called *Tuner.* The cedars were of enormous size ; one measured 18 cubits in girth at 4 feet from the ground, and was about 180 feet high ; another that had fallen down was 159 feet in length: and trees of this size were not uncommon. From this eminence I had a fine prospect, in which a cascade forming the source of the *Patal-Ganga*, that ran in the bottom between two ranges of hills, formed the most prominent feature. This cascade appeared to have a fall of from 80 to 100 feet and was about 20 feet broad. It had almost escaped me to remark, that in our return we met with very large Service trees, bearing fruit much larger than those of this tree in England. I stopped to examine some plants of hemp sown near a house ; many

5. Pine

of these were twelve feet in height, and few lower than ten ; where thinly sown, the plants had very thick stems and sent out many side branches ; but when numerous, they were thin, tall and without branches. The person, who sowed them, said, that when the plant was supposed sufficiently ripe for pulling, which is considered to be the case when it is in flower, it is placed on the roof of the house, and exposed to the sun till thoroughly dry ; when the bark is stripped off and tied in bundles for use. During the time it is on the house, care is taken to prevent its being wetted, as wet is supposed to weaken the fibres. In stripping, one half of the bark is separated from the wood, by the nails of the finger and thumb of one hand, whilst the finger and thumb of the other are placed, one upon and the other under the bark, during the time that it is drawn from the but towards the point of the stem : this process is performed on the other side and the bark by the two operations is completely taken off. From what I have seen of the growth of hemp in this country, I have no hesitation in saying that its luxuriance is such, when sown upon the lands of valleys in *Garwhal* and *Pain-khandi*, as to be capable of supplying a great portion of the navy of *Great Britain*, if its value in *England* will cover the freight and other expenses.

September 24th.—The Negi's mother last night informed us that Jawahir Singh had absconded as well as Bhawani Singh, in order to avoid the oppression of the *Gorkiahs.* She gave an afflicting statement of the grievances inflicted by them; assured us, that our loads should be forwarded, and that Bhawani Singh would not be faithless to his engagements : but that we should not see him, as both he and Jawahir feared to be seized and sent to *Sirinagar*. She was very anxious to impress us with a belief, that the warmest wishes of the whole of her family were with us. We then desired Bandhu Thapa's son and the jamadar would come to our tent, and remonstrated with them on our situation. Bandhu Thapa's son and an old man his governor expressed their concern at the delay in our journey, and said they were ready to accompany us to *Pali*, where we should see Bandhu Thapa, and that we might rely upon it our effects should reach *Pali* within three days after our arrival. We were obliged to remain satisfied with this explanation, but said, that if we had not an account of the baggage being on the road to us in three days, we would certainly march.

September 25th.—As a person acquainted with the management of goats and the culture of the mountain rice would be useful in going to *Calcutta* with the former, and perhaps eventually to *England,* I gave the sum of thirty rupees for a slave offered to me by Jawahir Singh, who was apprehensive that he would be forcibly taken from him by the *Gorkhas* if he did not dispose of him.

September 26th.—The jamadar Jag-rup came to take leave. As I saw he expected a present, I filled a *China* box with five rupees in *Timashis* and gave it to him. He appeared highly gratified with this, and we saw no more of him.

At 9.15 left the village of *Solur.* At 8380 paces reach *Pankei-math.* The latter part of this journey was very embarrassing, as the rain now was continued and heavy. The path was covered with a glaced surface, so slippery, that few of the party escaped without one or more falls. When quite dark I reached the *Garul Ganga,* whose current dashed along with great impetuosity. Having safely reached the bank, we were involved in the deepest darkness, and could only ascertain that we were at the foot of a steep hill. Here we were obliged to wait about three quarters of an hour, till a light was brought which shewed a steep narrow path much obstructed by stones and long grass. With much trouble we collected the goats and forced them into the path ; but they frequently stopped. Not being able to get them on after a stop of unusual length, I endeavoured to pass through them, and when I got to the foremost rank, felt myself suddenly slip through the grass over a steep ledge, which came along the edge of the path, and down the face of a bank or precipice ; for the darkness prevented me from judging the extent of the danger. A tuft of grass, after I had a short fall, came between my legs, and in a few seconds more I found myself seated upon a stone as if upon a saddle, my feet not touching the ground. By dint of groping about, I found some stout tufts of grass a little above me and well within my reach. These proved firm and enabled me, by there being a succession of them, and by placing my toes against the face of the bank, to raise my head to the level of the path in the grass; and the hand of a servant drew me up.

September 27th.—Thermometer 60°. This is a deserted village called *Panki-Math*, situated on the top of a hill, but surrounded, except towards the river, by an amphitheatre of others still higher. Bandhu Thapa's son's party had turned out the inhabitants of a village on the opposite side of the *Garul Ganga*, and taken refuge from the rain of last night in their houses. I thought it right to halt. Thermometer 67°. At four P.M. the son of Bandhu Thapa and his party, marched to *Pipal Koti* today, and was soon followed by Jagrup jamadar and his party.

September 28th.—Thermometer 53°. At 1462 paces reach the steps, which in going up, were an object of terror; but which now surprise us that we should have thought them formidable : this change in our sentiments has been worked by our having become familiar with worse roads, and likewise by the declivity being concealed by grass. Encamp at *Purut-kothu*, at 1.45, distance 3225 paces. The *Gorkhas* wished us to pitch close to a small house or fort, they were preparing to command the road to *Bhadrinath*, and that of the *Jhula* across the *Alacananda* to *Bandhath*, and the temple of *Kedarnath*. The invitation was declined for obvious reasons.

September 29th.—Halt this day. We are told that on the summits of the neighbouring mountains there was a large red tiger, which feeds on elks and the largest kind of game, but seldom comes to the lower part of the country. He is described to be of the size of a small horse, his neck is covered with hair so long as to fall over his face and almost conceal his head, as he comes down hill. From this account, it is presumable that the animal is a lion.

September 30th.—Thermometer 60° ; noon, 78° ; right, 68°. This land was given by the *Rajas* in *Jaghir* to *Bhadrinath* for the maintenance of the officiating priests ; and the *Gorkhas* have not disturbed the tenure, through they live at free quarters upon the farmers, when they come either to collect rents in the neighbourhood or for any other purpose, as in the present instance, when a force is collected to impose upon us a belief of their strength.

6

JOURNEY TO LAKE MANSAROVAR : THE MONTH OF OCTOBER

October 1st.—Bhawani Singh, by message through Harkh Deo, requested us to be particularly on our guard against treachery, which he apprehended would be employed against us. The *Gorkhalis* having sent some coolies, we marched with due precaution, our fire arms loaded, at half past two. At 1135 paces encamp on a narrow plot of grass formerly cultivated.

October 2nd.—Thermometer at sun-rise 51° ; noon 82° ; night 61°. This day about 11°, the subadar came to pay us a visit. He is a relation of the deposed *Palpa Raja.* It is worthy of notice, that two thirds of the troops of Bhacti Thapa, consist of the natives of the sub-jugated countries.

October 3rd.—Intermitment fevers are very common at this season, and attributed by the inhabitants to the rain which falls almost continually at the end of *Bhadon,* and the great moisture of the soil. But to the humidity of the atmosphere and the ground, may be added, the vegetable trash, they eat, and the close and filthy state of their houses, and especially the accumulation of all kinds of dirt round their habitations,

October 4th.—Went, accompanied by a few *Gorkha sipahis*, in pursuit of bears ; saw and wounded several.

October 5th.—A letter had come from Bandhu Thapa stating, that as he desired much to meet us, he wished we would march as soon as possible, and he would wait for us at *Chandpur*.

October 6th.—No coolies came. The jamadar said, we should certainly have them the following day.

October 7th.—Thermometer 60°. At 9 begin our march. As I thought it probable, that I should not be able to overtake the goats before night, and as the road was bad, and the sky looked wild and threatening, I endeavoured, as I passed some rocks, to find out some cavern in which I might take up my lodging, for the carriers were so far behind as to leave me little hope of their arriving with any bed. I saw at a distance from the road a deep recess in the face of the rock, and congratulating myself on my good luck, went to examine it more closely, when I suddenly felt an offensive smell, and proceeding to the cave, found the dead body of a man. In what manner he came by his death, I could not learn from the appearances about him : but, as he was not stripped and had white clothes, I suppose he was some pilgrim from *Hindustan*. At 8900 paces, I found the goats on a sandy and stony part of the bed of the *Alacanandra*. My bed arrived about ten o'clock, and my tent in the middle of the night. The *Bichari* pretends to be our friend, and recommends us to be on our guard. We set fire to piles of firewood, in order to keep off the leopards.

October 8th.—Thermometer 56°. March at 9. The deserted condition of the villages threatens this unfortunate country with the loss of all its inhabitants, if it remain under the dominion of the *Gorkhalis*. It is odd enough that every governor, and indeed every *sipahi*, sees what is to happen, but no one seems to make any attempt, on principle, to check the threatened depopulation. The governors of the different districts remain in them but for a few years, and it appears a maxim with them to make hay whilst the sun shines, whatever ills befall the unfortunate *rayat* from their exactions. Thermometer at night 65°.

October 9th.—Thermometer 59°. It began to rain briskly soon after I commenced my march, and continued two-thirds of the way. The road lay through a country, that once was highly cultivated, but which exhibits now little more than traces of what it has been. This day I found two men under the *Pippal* tree near the *Nandakni*, who wished to become my servants : one of these was a one-eyed fellow who had assisted in carrying our loads from *Najibabad.* As they seemed strong enough to be useful as carriers, and said they were starving in this country, had no connexions, having lost their wives, I took them into employ. Having mentioned the general features of the country, we went through this day, in our route upwards, it is unnecessary to say more than that the luxuriant vegetation had so altered its face in many places, as to render it a work of some time to recognise them. After a very complete wetting, the feel of the sun which showed itself nearly unclouded, near *Karn Prayag*, was not unacceptable. We reached the *Pindar-Ganga* at 6357 paces, when we crossed the *Jhula.* On the opposite side, on a stone *Chabutra,* under a *Pippal* tree, we found Bandhu Thapa, who rose at our approach. He is a stout old man of seventy, plain in his manners and dress, and altogether not superior in his appearance to one of the *zamindars* of *Ghazipur.* He sent word by the *Bichari,* that when we had eaten and taken some rest, he would wait on us. He came in the evening accompanied by the *Bichari* and the *Kamuniah.* On inquiring what were the motives for our passing through their country, we replied, that we wished to see the horses of the *Undes* and to procure some shawl wool goats. Why did we disguise ourselves ? To this it was answered, that he must well know it was the general custom of pilgrims so to do, but that we had a farther inducement, for, if this had not been done, we should not have been able to enter the *Undes,* as he must not be ignorant that all entrance to that country is interdicted to the *Gorkhalis* and to *Europeans* also. Why, he next asked, had we not applied for a *Parwana* ? Our answer was, that had we waited the time necessary for procuring a *Parwana,* the season for going through the *Himachal* would have passed ; but that had we found the horses required, we should have applied regularly for permission for going through the *Gorkhali* country. We then inquired, if he had to complain of our having committed any violence or irregularity in the course of our march. He answered in the negative. He was then informed, that hundreds of the *Nipalese* went through the Company's provinces in any direction they pleased without interruption. He admitted the truth of the remark, but said that he wished us to remain five days at *Karn-Prayag*, and afterwards said that this period might extend to fifteen or seventeen days, until a decision should be formed by the different chiefs as to the line of conduct to be taken. We said that we had been much detained at various places on different pretences, that our money was nearly exhausted, and that we could not make any further halt than one day, when we would proceed towards *Pali*, where we would halt two days. He said, that he was obliged to go to *Sirinagar*, on account of the *Dashara*, and we might not find any bearers the next day, but that we might depend upon them the following day ; and that he would order the *Bichari* to attend us to *Chilkiah*. We parted apparently on the best terms ; and Bandhu Thapa was much pleased with his present.

October 10th.—At 8 o'clock Bandhu Thapa set off in a *Dandi* or blanket, collected in gathers at the two ends and tied to a long pole. He was carried by two men, who must have been abundantly loaded, as he cannot weigh less than fifteen stone. The town of *Karn-Prayag*, contained many inhabitants in 1808 ; but, at present, a few *Brahmins*, who attend the temple, and some *mullahs* who take care of the *Jhula*, constitute the whole number.

October 11th.—Thermometer 55° ; noon 80° ; night 61°. After having completed 3358 paces in a southerly direction with some easting and westing, we encamed near a *Pippal* tree, having the *Pindar* on our left, and the *Chandpur* nullah emptying into this river in a broken stream a little before us, and about a quarter of a mile below our former ground of encampment. The soldiers along with us have scarcely any cartridges, and would have the worst of it, were they to attack us, but I trust this is not their intention, although I perceive their numbers are increased.

October 12th.—Thermometer 50° ; night 57°. A servant, I had brought from *Pipal Koti*, had been several times at *Adh-Bhadri*, and stated that the road on the right side of the *Chandpur* nullah was shorter and better than that by *Tope* or *Tamba Koti*, and that the people from this part of the country always went by this road. As it was a great object with me to save distance, I resolved to go by this road ; my companion determined to go by the other. I considered this a matter of little consequence, as the separation would only be for a few hours. Whilst on the road, a stout *Gorkhali*, whom I had not before seen, and who from his dress appeared of a rank superior to the rest, spoke to me in a very insolent tone, and placed himself in a menacing position, striking his musket violently against the ground. I snatched my gun from my servant, cocked it, and stopped with the intention of shooting him if he advanced a single step towards me. Another soldier, seeing what I was about, ran, begged me to desist, and abused the man who had been impertinent. The village was on a very high spot. I left my goats a few yards behind, and with my *Khalasi*, Cheta, went into a square flagged, on two sides of which were low buildings for cattle, and in front a high *Chabutra* connected with some houses. On the edge of this stood twentyfive *Gorkhali Sipahis*, principally new faces, and on the flags below were my loads. I asked who was the head of this force, and, on his being pointed out, asked him what was the meaning of this deception. He said it was expected that I should halt there, and every thing was ready for my accommodation ; I told him, that it was my intention to cross the *Chandpur*, nullah, that night, and desired to know if he meant to furnish bearers. He answered, that no bearers were to be had, and that it was impossible from the lateness of the hour to reach *Chandpur*. I saw that nothing was to be expected in the way of aid. A guide was even refused. I, therefore, ordered my people to throw away my things of least value, divide the rest, and march. Well aware that it would be impossible for me to reach the banks of the nullah, as the night was setting in, I pitched my tent on an elevated spot close to the *Math*. I placed a sentry on each road, and had a fire made sufficiently large to throw light upon them. My men were placed upon the *Chabutras*, and altogether my position was more respectable than could be expected on such an emergency. The fakirs, who live at the *Math*, desired us to be watchful, as a very large tiger had lately taken off three men from that neighbourhood.

October 13th.—The night has passed in quiet. I marched about 9, and in about an hour over a descending and slippery road came to the steep bank of a water course ; Mr. H. sent a note, stating that he had been stopped at the village of *Tope* yesterday, and desired to go to where I was. This he refused, and by shewing a firm determination to proceed was not opposed, but the *Gorkhalis* left behind, at the moment of his going on, were busily engaged in putting flints in their guns. He had reached *Adh-Bhadri*, was under arms and desired me to join him as soon as possible. In about an hour, I found Mr. H. encamped in some flat ground between the temples of *Adh-Bhadri* and a nullah. In a short time the carriers from *Bandoli*, most probably instructed by the *Gorkhalis*, all at once started up and ran off. It is believed, that this was done to delay our marching. We here disencumbered ourselves of the least valuable of our property, and divided the rest amongst our servants to carry. In the evening we set off. The *Gorkhalis* soon followed us. We were overtaken just as on the point of leaving our ground, by Harkh Deo, who said Kanak Singh was in the rear of the loads, which moved very slowly. We reached the *Mallsi* mulberry tree. The *Gorkhalis* encamped about a hundred yards above us. The march of this morning was about 4000 paces, that of the evening 2500.

October 14th.—Thermometer 48°. At 3500 paces I reached the summit of *Dewali-kalki Ghati*, having for the last mile proceeded through a fine forest of horsechesnut, walnut, ilex and rhododendron of the red kind. Many people have, it is said, been killed by tigers at this spot, within the last three months. At 5058 paces, cross the rivulet. Here we stopped to eat some *dal* and rice. Instead of stopping near us, as heretofore, the *Gorkhalis* proceeded about two miles in front to dress their victuals, and to make arrangements for stopping us at the *Sobha* pass. Had we not been embarrassed by our goats, a march across the *Gadra* to the right, leaving the *Ramganga* to the left, and steering towards *Langur* green, would have completely disconcerted their schemes, and have brought us into Mr. H's *jaghir* near *Laldang*. However, circumstanced as we were, it only remained for us to persevere, until we should have gained the *Sobha* pass, beyond which it would be difficult for them to stop us. After taking our frugal meal we proceeded. The distance from our halting-place is 2600 paces, and we encamped upon a flat on the left bank of the river, where we were met by some *Domes* with musick. At night a farmer brought his son that was sick, and expressed his concern at our situation, believing us in confinement. When it was explained that this was not the case, he said, that it must happen, as all the troops were to meet at *Sobha*, and detain us there, as they had failed of effecting their purpose before. Orders had been issued to all the farmers to assist them, in case we should resist them. Here again our escort departed for the night to a village at a distance, and had we not had the goats, we might have availed ourselves of this opportunity ; but I had determined, as long as it might be in my power, not to quit the animals which it had cost me so much pains to obtain.

October 15th.—Hoar frost, thermometer 47°. I marched with the goats. After having gone about a mile, I observed, that I had passed on the right, and below me, a body of about 80 or 100 men armed with muskets. They were evidently surprised, and hurried much to overtake me. I fell to the rear of the goats and continued my pace ; a man asked me where Hearsey sahib was, and desired me to stop. I asked him who he was, and by what authority he took the liberty of interrogating me. He replied that he was the jamadar of the party, and was sent to prevent our proceeding until his subadar and the principal zemindars of the country have a meeting with us. I told him, that I was proceeding quietly on the high road, molesting no one ; that I expected not to be molested, and that I should resist in the best way I could any attempt to stop me by force. That we had promised Bandhu Thapa to stay two days at *Pah*, and that we should stay that time according to our word. He then dropped his tone, and requested me to order my people not to go on, which I refused. As the soldiers had gathered round me, and were closing, I told him that if he did not order them to go to a distance, I should consider myself attacked and act accordingly ; and advised him to reflect on the consequences which might ensue by his forcing me to, defend myself. He ordered the soldiers to keep farther off. I continued to march, followed by the whole of the party. After reaching the bank of the river which was forded, a man of Bandhu Thapa's party came to know if I wished the goats to be carried ; for this civility, I thanked him, but declined giving him any trouble, save that if any of the goats should chance to be carried down the stream, that he would order his men to stop them just above a rapid at a short distance. I continued my march, when the jamadar said that if I would stop only one day, opposite Sumeru's house, the meeting would take place, and we might proceed. I refused to stop any where short of *Mehelchowri.* In half an hour more I saw a large new house half way up the hill on the right, and on the plain close by the road the party of soldiers was assembled, they having preceded me from our last conversation; a tall man, whom I understood to be Sumeru, came forwards, made a salam, spread a blanket and begged I would go to his village until the subadar should come. I said that I was upon the principal road ; and I was determined not to leave it until I should arrive at *Mehelchowri*. He requested me to stay only one day, during which the business would be settled. I told him we had been much deceived before, and at *Pali* only would we halt willingly. I resolved to wait for my companion coming up, that we might defend ourselves with more advantage against the force which now amounted to as much as the country could muster. Wishing likewise to draw Sumeru away, I gradually, whilst conversing, walked back again and he followed. At a proper place the note from D.S. was given. He said he knew its contents, and would furnish provisions and bearers, if we would only stop one day. In a short time Mr. H. came up ; he was of opinion, we ought to get beyond the *Sobha* pass, as if they failed to stop us there they could not have an equal opportunity elsewhere. I agreed with him and took charge of the advance, whilst he brought up the rear.

The goats were with me. A body of *Sipahis* ran before to gain a narrow part, which confined the path. One went through the goats ; I followed to push him from amongst them, and found about twenty men had formed a line upon the path. The man I had pursued, probably exasperated by being obliged to run in the sight of his countrymen, put himself in a menacing position on the path. I retired a few paces, dropped on one knee, in order to get a steady and low aim, when another advanced humbly, and the person, who appeared so resolute, threw down his musket and presented his neck also. I ordered the soldiers to quit the path, and they drew up on the side for me to pass. Whilst this was going on, Mr. H. was engaged in warm conversation with the *Sipahis* behind, had formed his few men into two divisions, and agreed to no other terms than those I had before proposed, viz., that we would go to *Mehelchowri* and wait there the remainder of the day. To this place we went ; and, having only made 4500 paces, encamped under the shade of a mulberry tree and salinga tree, close to the habitation of a *Gosain*. This personage was tall, thin, with a long beard and about eighty years of age. He approached with much respect, and desired me to sit down on part of the *Chabutra* under the mulberry, surrounded by stone figures of deities. In a short time bringing a pomegranate, he particularly requested that we would stay a few days, as violence would certainly be offered if we did not. He represented himself to be an inhabitant of *Oude* ; and, after residing here forty years, was anxious to die at *Benares*. He was tired of living in a country where religion was neglected, and every thing tended to desolation. In the evening a *Brahman* who was called a major, and who we understood executed the writing business belonging to the Company, now made his appearance with a message from the subedar, stating that today he was much engaged in ceremonies of ablution and worship, but that early in the morning he would certainly wait on us. To this we replied, that we had made a very short march to accommodate him, that he had not come agreeable to his promise, and that if he were disposed to see us, we would wait for him at the *Khutsar Gudrah*, on the south of the *Sabha* pass. The major represented, that it would much gratify him and the whole party, if we would stop here four or five days. This we positively refused. The old pandit was very desirous of our stay ; but, as we plainly perceived that time was all the subadar wanted, we resolved to persevere. The appearance of one of Mr. Rutherford's agents, who said he was come on his master's business, makes us disbelieve the report of there being any rupture between our government and the *Gorkhalis*, and makes us still more desirous to avoid actual hostilities.

October 16th—Morning very foggy. Thermometer 52°. We were stirring very early, and as the *Gorkhalis* were round us in considerable bodies, I had my breakfast placed on a stone and ate it, with my gun in my hand. Many jamadars and havildars came round Mr. H's tent, and the soldiers closed. I called to the principal jamadar and said if the soldiers did not immediately retire, I should look upon their presence as an hostile aggression and act in consequence. Seeing me thoroughly prepared, several of the officers came, offered their necks and desired me to take off their heads, as if they did not stop us that would be their fate : observing that many had got round me, I stepped away from them and the servants who had been sent off with the goats, said they were not allowed to proceed. I then saw that a body of about thirty had barred the path, were forming in a semicircle, and coming on to attack us. I called to my companion to prepare, and sprung into the path, desiring the soldiers to stand clear. The main body opened a little, and I independently advanced with too much impetuosity. A man or two advanced, and I shoved them back. My gun had in an instant as many hands upon it, as could find room to touch it, but they could not wrest it from me. I had at least seventeen or twenty upon me but this rather prolonged than shortened the contest, as they pulled in opposite directions. It would have been maintained for even a longer time, had not one man got upon my neck and stuck his knees into my loins, endeavouring to strangle me with my handkerchief, whilst another fastened a rope round my left leg and pulled it backwards from under me. Supported only by one leg and almost fainting from the hand round my neck. I lost my hold on the gun, and was instantly thrown to the ground. Here I was dragged about by the legs until my arms were pinioned. When I had got up, nothing could surpass the savage expression of joy depicted in the countenance of the victors, nor was the ferocity of their actions much behind-hand. For fear of my getting loose, two soldiers held me fast by a cord and every now and then gave me a violent jerk by way of letting me know my situation. I desired to be placed upon the *Chabutra* out of the crowd and, after some hesitation, this was complied with. Mr. H., it seems, had little suspicion of so immediate an attack, as he was washing his mouth when the affiray begun and did not hear my call to him. Our servants were absent from the small pile of arms we had, I had only one armed man in my suite, having given over my other double-barrelled gun to Mr. H. for hir own immediate use ; and to my servant who had a long duck gun, I had given the most express orders not to fire unless the *Gorkhalis* fired first. Mr. H. and the whole of our servants, except two or three who escaped this fate, I know not how, were secured ; Mr. H. was not bound but secured by persons holding his arms. Some of the others were struck with the butt ends of muskets and much maltreated. In about two hours, during which I remained bound, the subadar made his appearance. He seemed quite a beau, just stepping from his toilette, saluted all the soldiery with a simpering smile of exultation playing on his countenance. He did not deign to salute either Mr. H. or myself, and we were certainly not in the humour to pay any compliments. After casting upon us some looks of survey, he retired to hold a council. In a few minutes he came again, and having a carpet spread near Mr. H., seated himself upon it and entered into conversation. I asked him whether the rope ornaments placed round my arms were the bands which connected the friendship of the *English* and the *Gorhhalis* ? Whether this was a conduct that was justifiable towards a traveller who entered into the country peaceably, who had demeaned himself in the most peaceable manner whilst he remained in it, and was returning peaceably towards his own home ? To this he asked, why I went through the country in disguise? I answered, to avoid expense, unnecessary delay, and to enable me to get into the *Undes*. During this time I remained bound. He desired me to be seated : this I refused until the cords were taken off my arms ; which he ordered. The excuse he urged for not coming before, was that the day was one of great religious ceremony, if so, I observed, what reason was there for his having delayed not making his appearance till so late an hour, it being now near twelve. He stammered out some imperfect apology. I pointed out the bound people and desired that either they might be unbound or that I might be re-shackled. He said that they all should be set at liberty, and two or three were loosed. In about half an hour the subadar left us, and after a long consultation, in which jamadars havildars and sipahis bore a part, a letter was written to Bam Sah at *Almora*. This cowardly fellow had prudently kept himself out of the way, till the scuffle was over. By acting as we have done, we have got into a part of the country less remote from the plains, and more in the way of sending information of what has occured. In the evening, our low country servants were unbound, but those we have hired to bring on our baggage, were still bound, as well as the *Pandit* and his nephew. The former acted with firmness, the latter was much cast down. I desired that some of my servants might go to attend my goats. This was acceded to. On looking over the events of this day and reflecting on the consequences which may result from them, I cannot but be grateful to the Author of all, for having given me firmness to bear my present situation without the dread of the death, now likely to cut short my career. About fifty people are set to guard us ; and they are so noisy as to afford little chance of sleep to-night.

October 17th.—This day was ushered in by the hammering of a blacksmith preparing fetters. In the forenoon, the two *Pandits* were taken away as we apprehended, to be put to the torture ; however, in this we were mistaken, as it was for the purpose of placing one leg in a square hole cut of a heavy log of wood, and a strong peg being driven across the two sides of the notch retained the foot. Several of my servants were shackled in this manner ; and of Mr. H's. One of my bearers offered to carry a letter, as also did my goatherd. This man came up as a fakir, the second day after we had come over the *Niti* pass, and said he would take service, provided I would furnish him with victuals till we should reach the plains. He purposed going to the subadar, saying that he was a fakir, had only accompanied us for his victuals, and wished to depart. If he got permission, he said he knew what road to go by, to prevent being stopped at any of the *Gorkhali chokis*; and should, bating accidents, reach *Chilkaih* on the third day. I wrote a letter to Sir E. Colebrooke, open, relating the general circumstances of our situation, and that the only matter which could be laid to our charge, was going through the country in *Hindu* dresses. This, along with one from Mr. H. to his brother-in-law, Lieutenant Salmon, were put into a piece of my orange-coloured mantle and sewn within the doubles of an old woollen wrapper, in which the fakir kept the instruments he used in prayer. He made his representation to the subadar, but was ordered back into confinement. This did not disconcert him. He was confident that he should be able to execute the commission he was charged with. He said that he had eaten my salt, would not be ungrateful; that he should not stop here, but having his beard shaved and having changed his dress, he should proceed with an answer to *Almora* or wherever we might be. He left me, and I suffered an hour to elapse before I looked for him. He was then sitting down on the ground with his blanket on his head and arranging some wood in a bundle, as if for cooking. When another hour had passed again, I saw the heap of wood with a bundle of clothes laying by it, close to one of the sentries, but the fakir had disappeared. Should he succeed we owe him great obligation as the probability of our deliverance depends almost entirely on the representation Sir E. Colebrooke will make to the chief of *Almora*. We desired the subadar to allow the major to write a letter from us jointly to the *Choutra*, Bam Sah, stating in general terms, that as we had been imprisoned and bound by his order, we desired to be taken to *Almora*. We enclosed a note to Mr. Hawkins, mentioning the imprisonment and requested the *Choutra* to forward it to that gentleman. I gave the major a pair of scissors for his trouble and a rupee to each of the two soldiers, who were going to *Almora* with the letter. A reward of three more was promised if they brought us an answer on the fourth day. A considerable number of farmers was brought together by order of the subadar, in order to show them the punishment he had inflicted on the *Sahiblog*, commiseration was depicted in their countenances, which formed a striking contrast with those of our guards. The old *Gosain* continues his kindness in bringing all the milk his cow gives, morning and night. This is very little, but it shews his will.

October 18th.—About 10 o'clock, the fakir was missed. A great noise was made ; and a strict search for about an hour ; and persons sent out in every direction ; however, I trust that our messenger will have got completely out of their reach, This escape has made them doubly vigilant, and a man looks into the tent every hour at least.

October 19th.—The old *Pandit*, his nephew and our hill servants were released from their logs, but had their hands bound and were taken away to *Almora.* To the *Pandits* I gave presents of money, and an order for a further sum on my agent ; and in the event of their deaths, I made a provision from my effects for the maintenance of their families. We were told that our low country servants should now be released from their logs. An abbatis of stakes interwoven with brush wood was made round, The stakes, being only driven straight down, might easily be drawn up. I mention this because, after the *Gorkhalis* have made an attack, they usually entrench themselves in this manner.

October 20th.—Thermometer 45°.

October 21st.—The fogs are said to hang over the *Ramganga* at this season, for about half this month : when they disperse, they are very dense and penetrating. One of the hill servants I hired as a cooly on the banks of the *Nandakni* arrived with his load. He had been sick and obliged to stay at a village behind. The other man Tilak, now gone to *Almora*, said that we might rely upon his honesty and fidelity, and he has given a proof of it, as, if he had been dishonest, he might have gone off with his load unmolested, but though evincing some little courage in coming to persons in captivity, after learning the fate of his comrade, we find it is confined to this, for on sounding him as to taking a letter to *Moradabad*, he expressed his fears, and though apparently recovered, cited his illness as one cause for his not undertaking the journey.

October 22nd.—Our servants were this day released from their logs and had more liberty allowed them for moving about. Seventh day of imprisonment.

October 23rd.—In the evening the two jamadars arrived with a letter from Bam Sah. This acknowledged the receipt of our letter and a copy of an order from *Nipal*, stating that having heard that two persons had gone towards the *Undes* in disguise with guns, &c., Bandhu Thapa was ordered to stop them on their return and know their business, and who they were, and also to detain them till an answer should be received from *Catmandu*. The jamadars said they were surprised we had gone privately when we might have commanded the country. We returned the same answer as to Bandhu Thapa, that it was to avoid delay and inconvenience ; but from all I have seen, I am thoroughly convinced that if we had applied for permission, it would not have been granted.

October 24th.—The jamadars who brought the letter from Bam Sah, came this morning to say that they had orders to procure whatever we might stand in need of. The jamadars pretended to express astonishment at the severity of the usage we had met with, which they said was not agreeable to the orders the subadar had received, and stated that this had not been reported to Bam Sah.

Octboer 25th.—A letter to Bam Sah was finished and sealed. We determined to send Kangh Singh with it, that we might be sure of its reaching Bam Sah, and that he might fully represent the treatment we had experienced. A half kind of consent was given to this by the jamadars. A copy of our former dispatch to Sir E. Colebrooke, to which were added recent incidents, was given to the father of a boy, whom I had relieved by tapping for dropsy. He said that he should go to his house immediately, would place the letter in the sole of one of his shoes, and carrying these in his hand, would reach *Chilkiah* on the third day.

October 26th.—This evening we took a walk out of the northern gate of the abbatis, and prolonged it for about an hour in order to reconnoitre the adjacent country, for the purpose of attempting our escape should there appear a necessity for the measure. Our guards apparently did not miss us for the first half hour, when our absence gave them much alarm ; and suspecting we had actually effected our escape, people were sent out in every direction to apprehend us. The attempt to escape from hence would be difficult, as in such case we must proceed completely through the wildest part of the country : and almost all the small watercourses, by which the mountains are separated, serve as the retreat of bears and other wild beasts,

October 27th.—When we reached this place, the sides of the mountain were beautifully green but in this short space, by the night frosts, they have assumed the russet livery of autumn : so rapid is the change of season in this country.

October 28th.—Early this morning a jamadar came into our tent and seating himself, said the object of his journey was to convey us to *Sirinagar*, where Amr Singh wished us to be. This man brought no letter ; and his interference was evidently the cause of some perplexity to our jamadars. Amr Singh is the head of the army and Bam Sah, the chief of these districts.

October 29th.—The watchfulness of our guards has not in the least diminished. A zemindar brought to the troops some *Ghee* for sale. Some one complained that oil was mixed with it. The servant of the owner was laid hold of, and through fear of being punished, if he did not confess that his master had adulterated the *Ghee*, made an accusation to this effect. The supposed culprit was seized, stripped, bound and flogged severely with thongs. The *Ghee* was confiscated for the use of the soldiers ; and twentyfive rupees as a fine were ordered to be paid as the fine to the subadar. Should the poor wretch not be able to pay this in money, his cattle or children will be seized to the amount, and the value will be paid by the person who is to benefit by the property.

October 30th.—Today more troops reached us from *Sirinagar* ; and we have with us in all about 190 men.

October 31st—Another jamadar now came with a few men, saying that he had the orders of Bandhu Thapa to proceed with us to *Sirinagar*, from whence we were to go to *Haridwar* ; and that on the road we were to be met by Ranjur Kajee, the son of Amr Singh Although Bandhu Thapa did not write, we thought it right to send him a short letter, stating that as we now were on the high road to *Chilkia*, it would be highly inconvenient for us to leave it. This jamadar is about sixty, of a more frank character than any of his brethren we have met with, and is employed in going through the district to prevent the farmers running away. He said his efforts to give confidence to the farmers were ineffectual, and the orders of the *Raja* were disobeyed. An order had been issued under the great seal of the prince, in consequence of the great loss in the population of *Garhwal*, prohibiting the soldiers from taking any of the inhabitants as slaves : but this was wholly disregarded and the soldiers always escaped the punishment with which they had been threatened. Living in free quarters, without receiving any check for their conduct, the soldiers had, the old man observed, so far oppressed the country, that where there formerly twentyfive families, now only one was to be found.

7

JOURNEY TO LAKE MANSAROVAR : NOVEMBER 1ST TO NOVEMBER 5TH

November 1st—The jamadars from *Almora* came at an early hour, to report that orders had arrived from Bam Sah to return all the things which had been taken from us ; and after the lapse of about two hours, they returned with the guns, & c. We now found ourselves in the way to liberty and resolved not again to part with our arms except with our lives. This day our hill servants arrived. The old *Pandit* and his nephew were in irons, but were furnished with victuals by Bam Sah.

November 2nd.—Hoar frost. Thermometer 36° ; night 60°. We made preparations for marching at 9.15, left *Mehelchowri* and ascended the *Sobha* pass. At the foot of the descent from the *Sobha* pass is the *Khatsur* valley, and half way down is a knoll of calcareous rock, the western side of which, about thirty feet high, and over-hanging the base, forms a shallow cavern attributed to one of the *Surs*. From chinks in the stone exudes a small quantity of black bitumen. The *Khatsur* valley is about a mile broad : in the middle the edges are full of springs, the water of which is collected for irrigating the flats. This valley produces the *Bansmati* rice, next in quantity to that of *Chukam*, and would give vast crops of hemp of the finest quality. We pitched on a rice flat, on the right bank of the *Ramganga*, opposite to a small village called *Jhatah*. Kangh Singh overtook us here with a letter from Bam Sah, stating that his son was on the road to meet us ; that our ill treatment did not proceed from him and that the authors of it should be severely punished.

November 3rd.—Thermometer 41° ; night 69°. March at 10 ; we encamped under a *Pipal* tree a little below *Mashi*, on the left bank of the *Ramganga*. The top of *Ghensali ka Ling*, covered with snow, was very visible in a northern direction. Our supposed march today about seven miles. There was here an immense quantity of fish. The people place loose bundles of rice straw in the river and keep them down with large stones The fish, coming into them to deposit their spawn, are seized by the hand before they can get from within the straw. In front up the hills are three ovens for extracting tar ; but the pines are small, and of course do not contain much turpentine.

November 4th.—Thermometer 50° ; night 62°. The son of Bam Sah was announced just as we had finished dinner : when he came, preceded by an old man repeating his titles, & c., and five or six bazar girls. His name is Lachbir Sah, about twenty-six or twentyeight years of age. He was dressed in fine *Dacca* muslin, and had about twenty shabby orderlies in attendance. He expressed the concern his father was under, at learning how we had been treated, and was anxious to have us believe that the *Sipahis* had acted not only without his father's orders but even without any orders at all, He appeared desirous, we should say we forgave what had happened, and the persons who had committed the outrage should be punished, we requested that the *Pandits* might be released, and stated that we were unwilling that servants should be punished, for having acted agreeably to their orders. Lachbir Sah said that he would make a severe example of the soliders who had been most active in seizing us, if we would point them out. It was obviously his intention to have given up a few of these wretches to condign punishment, in order that we might have the odium and consequences of the act, and that his government might retaliate upon the *Pandits*. It was stated by us that we should derive no pleasure or satisfaction from the immediate agents being punished ; but we should be glad to know the authors of our arrestation, who were principally to blame ; and we further said that as far as we were concerned we should forgive the men, provided the *Pandits* were immediately returned, so as to quit the country with us. He said he would write this proposition that evening to his father, and wished us to stay till a messenger should return from *Almora* with an answer. He said that Dasrath Bakshi had written to *Nepal* that we had taken up between 4 and 500 men with muskets, &c., had erected forts on the border between *Bothant* and the *Undes*, and were endeavouring to raise the *Marchas* and *Unias* against the *Gorkhalis.*

November 5th.—The jamadars last night requested that the subadars might be furnished with a certificate of their good conduct toward us. We said that we had no objection to give a certificate of the good behaviour of the one, and that we pardoned the other, provided he would ask pardon of the old *Pandit* for the treatment he had experienced from him and his soliders. Lachbir Sah came in the afternoon and announced receipt of a letter from the *Raja* of *Nepal*, ordering us to be seen safe out of the country with all our effects, and that we should be treated with civility, He observed we were at liberty to depart whenever we might think proper.

INDEX

Alacananda 1, 119, 121
Almora 3, 131-133, 137, 139
Amer Singh 26, 30, 33, 34, 40-42, 47, 93, 135

Baral 23, 36, 39, 54, 55, 71, 75, 107
Benares 64, 128
Bhadrinath 1, 63, 104, 119
Bhawani Singh 114, 116, 117
Butan 16, 17, 27, 100, 101, 106, 108, 113

Cailas 35, 39, 76, 83, 86
Cedar and Cypress 3, 9, 12
Chasmirian 59, 60, 64-65, 97, 99
Chilkiah 134, 136
Colebrooke 1, 77, 132, 134

Daba 19, 23-26, 31, 37, 39, 40, 44, 49, 52, 53, 57, 58, 63, 64, 96
Dauli 1-3, 6, 11, 12, 15, 27, 30-32, 101, 102, 104, 105, 108-111, 113
Deba 23-26, 41-43, 45, 50, 57, 58, 61, 63, 66, 67, 88, 94-96, 98-101, 112

Ganesa 15
Garpan 65, 69, 70, 87, 88, 94, 96, 97
Gelums 44, 47, 49, 51, 72, 79, 87, 95, 96
Ghertope 40, 42, 48, 49,56, 59, 63-68, 75, 93, 95, 98-100
Gillman, Mr. 66, 87
Gomasale 24-25
Gorkhas 118-120

Harballabh 77, 82,
Haridwar 77, 98, 136
Harkh Deo, Pandit 1, 98, 125
Hawkins, Mr. 132
Hearsay, Mr. 1, 3, 8, 14, 77, 126

Joshi Math 1, 16, 17, 107, 110, 114, 115
Jowar Singh 3, 112

Karn Prayag 122
Kazalbash, Ahmed Khan 65
Kedarnath 119
Kien-Lung 88-90

Lamak 23, 40-43, 45-49, 51, 52, 66, 72, 74, 78, 79, 81, 82
Latak 56, 59-61, 64, 65

Malari 13-15, 17, 24, 108-110, 112, 113

Mansarovar 18, 19, 24-25, 35, 40, 47, 59, 75, 76, 81-87, 100
Mapang 75, 77, 83
Marchas 17, 23, 30, 114-116, 139
Moorcroft, Mr. 204

Nerba 71, 72, 88
Niti 101, 20-25, 27, 29-31, 114
Niti Ghati 33, 100, 109

Pind-Ganga 122, 123

Ramganga 126, 133, 138
Raper 77
Rauni 5
Rutherford, Mr. 129

Sanga 2, 5, 9, 10
Sehana 19, 23
Singh, Deba 97, 99, 100
Sirinagar 3, 113, 117, 123, 135, 136
Sobha Pass 125-128, 137

Tapoban 3, 4, 6, 16, 63
Tatar 16, 41, 48, 51, 57, 58, 65, 68, 76, 77, 84, 97 ; Tatary 37, 41, 67, 71, 92
Tiltil 44, 52, 99
Tirtapuri 72, 74, 87-89

Undes 19, 23-24, 30, 32, 40, 60, 63, 65-66, 87, 91, 93, 102, 108, 113-114, 122, 131, 134, 139
Uniyas 19, 23, 24, 34, 35, 37-39, 59, 60, 77, 88, 90, 95, 101, 104, 109, 139

Vishnu Ganga 1

Wazir 40, 41, 43, 45, 48, 50, 57, 58, 61, 62, 66, 67, 94-99, 101, 102
Webb 77